THE CORE

THE CORE

Teaching Your Child the Foundations of Classical Education

Leigh A. Bortins

THE CORE
Copyright © Leigh A. Bortins, 2010.
All rights reserved.

First published in 2010 by PALGRAVE MACMILLAN® in the United
States–a division of St. Martin's Press LLC, 175 Fifth Avenue, New York, NY
10010.

Where this book is distributed in the UK, Europe and the rest of the world,
this is by Palgrave Macmillan, a division of Macmillan Publishers Limited,
registered in England, company number 785998, of Houndmills, Basingstoke,
Hampshire RG21 6XS.

Palgrave Macmillan is the global academic imprint of the above companies and
has companies and representatives throughout the world.

Palgrave® and Macmillan® are registered trademarks in the United States, the
United Kingdom, Europe and other countries.

ISBN 978-0-230-10035-0

Library of Congress Cataloging-in-Publication Data
Bortins, Leigh A.
    The core : teaching your child the foundations of classical education /
Leigh A. Bortins.
        p.   cm.
    Includes index.
    ISBN 978-0-230-10035-0 (pbk.)
        1. Classical education—United States—Handbooks, manuals, etc.
    2. Education, Humanistic—United States—Handbooks, manuals, etc.
    3. Home schooling—United States—Handbooks, manuals, etc.
    4. Education—Parent participation—United States—Handbooks, manuals,
    etc.   I. Title.
    LC1011.B615   2010
    370.11'2—dc22

                                                                    2009052000

A catalogue record of the book is available from the British Library.

Design by Letra Libre, Inc.

First edition: June 2010

10 9 8 7 6 5 4

Printed in the United States of America.

Dedicated to my son, John

CONTENTS

ACKNOWLEDGMENTS

As I went through the process of finishing this book, I read Stephen King's book *On Writing* and learned that we share two perspectives in common: *The Elements of Style* is the definitive guide for authors, and your editor is always right. As this was my first time working with an editor, I didn't know what to expect. But as we proceeded, I realized that Luba Ostashevsky was as interested in producing a well-received, intelligent book as I was. Luba took the time to listen to my perspectives and then help me come up with the best way of discussing classical education with a broad audience of parents. I am thankful that my agent, Andrew Stuart, tried very hard to understand the book's message and then found the right editor. I also want to thank my copy editor, Mark LaFlaur, for making my final edits clear through his interesting and helpful comments and corrections. I'm pleased with the whole Palgrave Macmillan team.

I also want to thank my assistant, Karen Hubbard, for so ably pretending to be me while I was writing, Jen Greenholt for double checking my resources as I wrote, and the whole Classical Conversations team, who went out of their way to relieve me of responsibilities so I could work on this book. I also appreciate the encouragement I received from Becky Norton Dunlop to reach out beyond the homeschooling community.

Mostly, I want to thank my children for thinking I have something worth saying and allowing me to practice ideas on them before I share them with the rest of the world. I like that you like to be with your parents and I pray that it's because our hearts are knit together and not just because your Dad and I are easy targets for your sharp wits. Thanks Rob for giving me a family that laughs a lot.

Leigh Bortins

PREFACE

The Core: Teaching Your Child the Foundations of Classical Education is:

For parents frustrated with their children's inability to reach their academic potential.

For stay-at-home moms and dads who want to homeschool.

For work-at-home parents who want to reinforce rigorous academics at home.

For principals trying to strengthen basic academics.

For school board members tired of seeing "innovative" curricula repeatedly fail children.

For employers wondering why *they* need to teach the basic skills to high school graduates.

For community leaders struggling to offer a low-cost, highly effective, private academy.

For adults frustrated by job displacement and ready to broaden their abilities.

For headmasters of classical schools frustrated by low
certification standards.

For teachers trying to teach rather than be surrogate parents.

For anyone trying to understand how to raise a generation of
capable thinkers and leaders.

The Core: Teaching Your Child the Foundations of Classical Education is not
just for families with a full-time, stay-at-home parent. Dual-income families want to be just as involved in their children's education as those who
have figured out how to survive on one income. Single parents need ideas
for their children's education that fit naturally into the limited time they
have together at home. Professional educators want to be able to give parents practical ways to help their children with homework. This book can
help anyone become more involved in raising not only academically successful students but also children enlivened by a genuine and enduring interest in learning.

FOREWORD

Education is the key that unlocks the door to infinite possibilities for everyone in a free society.

Family is the basic building block for success for human beings the world over. It is the unit designed to enable us to love, share, learn, grow, practice, and prosper in a secure place. Family ties are the most important relationships in the lives of boys and girls.

"Classic" describes something special, important, valuable, or authoritative. Something classic stands the test of time and sets a standard of excellence. Classic cars, classic music, classic literature . . . a classic education.

How-to books are popular and immensely useful to those who want help on a project important enough to them that they are willing to invest their own time and effort.

Take these four elements and weave them together and you have a beautiful tapestry for children—no, for *families* to experience. Differences, complex personalities, unique designs all integrated, producing a rich lifetime of loving and learning. Families thrive. Children excel.

Leigh Bortins has done exactly this in the book you hold in your hands. If you have children of your own—of any age—and you long for a way to be certain they will prosper in life, you will love this book. If you deal with children in an educational situation, this book will motivate you to think differently about how they might learn in the best possible ways. And, if you simply care about the children around you, in your neighborhood, in your church, in your extended family, or in the families of your coworkers, you will find this book personally inspiring and you will want to share it.

Debates over the best way to educate children have been going on for years and years. I personally have come to believe that public education has far too often eliminated parents from the equation. Naturally, the result is that parents are removed from knowing what their children are learning, how they are learning it, and what motivates the children to learn, as well as from knowing about key decisions in their children's educational life. This cannot be beneficial to the children, their parents, or the family. There is a better way, and in this book Leigh Bortins shares it clearly and concisely, and in a manner that reveals a lifetime of experience in, commitment to, and love for educating children.

The Core: Teaching Your Child the Foundations of Classical Education recognizes that for most children, public education remains the likely option . . . but it offers ideas and solutions that will enhance their chances for success. It envisions other alternatives and lays out the blueprint for more ways in which moms and dads can become their child's best teacher and strongest ally in preparation for life's journey. This book gives great encouragement to creative teachers and administrators who want to raise the standards, expectations, and results for their students.

What better could we do for the children than to motivate families to "get educated" together and encourage parents to help their youngsters; older children to help their younger siblings; and families to meet challenges together? Everyone in the family benefits, strengthening the family, community, and country.

I mentioned the importance of children prospering in life. "Prosperous" is a word that means something different depending on one's circumstances. And, in difficult times, challenging times, we all want to see a remnant that can provide enlightened leadership to their peers and to future generations. Reading this book is an important step to ensuring that you will be educating your family so that they will all be leaders who prosper no matter what the circumstances in their lives.

Leigh Bortins has written a classic. It is warm, funny, and engaging. So, read on, and prepare to see the opportunities emerge for your family on every page.

Becky Norton Dunlop, Vice President for
Outreach at The Heritage Foundation

INTRODUCTION

My husband, Rob, and I began homeschooling our children the moment our eldest son was born. We didn't necessarily think of ourselves as homeschoolers at the time, but, in hindsight, we see that every parent everywhere actually centers their children's education around the home. Whether we like it or not, we are our children's primary instructors and they learn the most from us. One of my worst moments as a parent is when I see my child acting inappropriately and I realize he is mirroring my own behavior. And conversely, of course, one of my greatest joys is when I see my child do something laudable and I know that it was thanks to something I taught him.

As our children matured—and my husband and I together with them—we advanced from informal homeschooling to modern schooling techniques. As our eldest two sons completed high school courses at home, they excelled on all the usual school things—standardized tests, papers, math assignments, sports, etc. When we would try to read the great works of literature such as classical literature, Shakespeare, and historical texts—the same documents that high school students used to study—something was not quite right. Our whole family could easily read the words, but none of us could fathom the meaning because we did not have the context for what was being said.

As my husband and I discussed the problem over the course of several years, our family expanded by two more sons, and we wanted to do a better job of educating them than we had with our first pair. Our search led us to the classical model of education that was practiced by scholars as long as there has been learning. The application and success of the model is not confined to a single time or place, though its name refers to the Greek and Roman eras. We discovered that wherever and whenever man had achieved high levels of literacy, the classical skills of grammar, dialectic, and rhetoric had been emphasized over job training or vocational studies. So we chose to travel down a new path, actually an ancient road, with our four boys. After much work, we discovered that we could participate in the conversations of mankind's greatest thinkers. Their words allowed us to more confidently confront the problems of daily living.

So now, our family reads literature together, such as George Herbert's poems and the U.S. Constitution, and we memorize large quantities of Latin vocabulary. It may seem strange that a present-day family headed by engineers with sons in technical fields chooses to cap off a day of designing machines or tackle football by reading the classics, but we feel more connected because of it. Not just connected to one another, but also to people we have never met. Our sense of the world is expanding. Now when we hear a new idea in politics we can recognize it as an old idea of Machiavelli's, for example. We can listen to political shows and shake our heads as we say in sorrow, "Ad hominem, ad hominem..." as pundits attack each other personally instead of critiquing each other's ideas.

Before I embraced the classical model, I felt I was living in the wrong century and with the wrong tribe. Classical studies introduced me to all of my lost relatives. I now feel that my sense of the world has grown by two thousand years. The voices from the past expand how I see and understand the world around me. I feel as though we hear a deeper, more confident voice and can respond in kind. While they are young, I want our four boys to learn the skills needed to hear the collective wisdom of the ages. I want them to regularly consult the advice of wise and virtuous men and women for their problems and predicaments today.

Parents and teachers ask me about classical education nearly every day. They know something is just not quite right with contemporary education, and they know it's not right because their child isn't learning as much or as well as he or she could. You know that education should connect your family to the best of history while preparing them for the future. The classical model provides insights not only into what your family could be learning, but also how to learn it. Then your family can also listen to the wisdom of the past, and their voices can help us evaluate our daily lives and see our place and purpose in a broader historical perspective.

Our family has been practicing the classical model of education since 1997, and we're almost good at it. I say "almost" because it's a work in progress. It has taken time and commitment and regular practice to bring the great classical conversations of humanity into our home, but I think it has been worth the effort. In one sense, we can't rewind time to make up for the lost years when we didn't educate classically, but here's the magic: the classical model allows one to learn forever. So our grown sons, who only had a few years of classical education at home (less time than our younger sons), steal our books to read in their own homes. And my husband and I get to fall in love again and again over poetry and passages of literature as we become old enough to be considered ancient ourselves. The lost years apart from our classical roots are being redeemed.

I believe all children deserve to receive a classical education. It's a "gift that keeps on giving" because it is double-pronged. Classical education emphasizes using the classical *skills* to study classical *content*. As the founder of Classical Conversations, a network of communities that use the classical model to teach at home, I speak to parents all over the country, teaching them how to implement the classical model at home. In one sense it is hard to do because it means entering an unfamiliar educational paradigm. On the other hand, once you begin to understand the nature of classical education and how well it trains the mind to think, learning becomes easier. I tell my children, "The fun's begun when the hard work is done."

This book will familiarize parents and educators not just with classics or a list of great books, but also with how to develop a classical education for your children. For me, it has been a humbling experience. I often have to forget all of my academic credentials and remember that when I am learning something new, I am only as smart as a first-grader. Fortunately, I'm more experienced and mentally agile than a first-grader, so I can quickly restore a lot of what I missed as a child. Our home-centered learning allows both my husband and me to recover the foundations of a classical education at the same time as our children.

The most important point I can make is that any parent who really tries can become more involved in his or her children's education. There are many families who like working and learning together. It is not always easy, but it is rewarding to guide your children's education. The first requirement is to believe that it is important and that you can do it. Whenever I hear a parent groan, "I could never homeschool my children" or "The classical model is too hard," I find I have to agree with them—not for everyone, but for those who lack confidence. The person who says, "I can" and the person who says, "I can't" are both right. I believe every parent *can* participate in the restoration of our culture to one that appreciates classical learning, but only if they will believe it about themselves. I believe the strong love of parents for their children makes them capable of providing a quality education for children centered from the home.

The Core: Teaching Your Child the Foundations of Classical Education begins at the beginning, with a grammar education for elementary students and parents. A grammar education is not really too hard to replicate, as it is designed for young students. The majority of this book describes techniques that I have developed for my children in order to form the basis of their grammar school education. This curriculum works for a student of any age, but that is a hard idea to digest because we think in terms of grade levels. I address each subject as though you would be teaching a child under thirteen, but then combine the discussion with ideas for older students and adults. As we get older, it is easier to assess the basic skills we are missing.

Through stories of real children studying quality content, we will grapple with the purpose and goals of education while providing copious examples for practical implementation. My hope is that not only parents but any adult concerned with the state of education will find this book useful.

Some of the terms I use need to be defined. I refer to today's education as "factory education" because, historically, the industrial age coincided with a national mandate to provide public education for the masses. In order to take on this enormous task, school systems replicated some of the efficiencies built into a large factory, as if they could ignore the fact that the "components" coming down the "assembly line" were children.

Some educators envision computers as the salvation of modern educational woes because they can be tailored to the individual child's needs. But the over-proliferation of computers in the classroom would render the warm touch of a teacher obsolete. I refer to the increasing use of computers in school as education in the age of global technologies. A classical education would embrace the efficiency of new technologies as they offer opportunities for individualized instruction, but would reject parallel monologue as a good form of education. Both factory and computer education rob a child of the need to think and replace loving, caring mentors with a machine or a system. The classical model emphasizes that learning feeds the soul and edifies the person rather than producing employees to work an assembly line. The goal of a classical education is to instill wisdom and virtue in people. We see learning as a continuing conversation that humankind has been engaged in for centuries, and we are concerned that industrialization and technologies reduce contact and context between children and their elders.

I know you are very likely shaking your head and saying that all of this is well and good, but how do I put this wonderful program into practice and how do I get my child to take part when we barely have time to tackle school assignments?

My answer would be to get back to basics. Your kids may be attending schools that have different expectations. Parents and educators know they need to work together to restore high academic expectations, but they aren't always sure where to make changes. I suggest they begin by thinking about modern education as a system of leveling. We have built factories of education where people other than parents control the purse strings and outcomes. Many books describe the problems with modern education, so I won't waste time repeating what has been said at length elsewhere. Instead, after devoting a chapter to summarizing the problems already mentioned, the main part of the book offers a time-tested solution.

Even children like mine who are homeschooled will attend schools of some kind throughout their lives. I want them to feel that it is a great advantage to attend a seminary, college, or trade school because the students who attend are equally interested in lifelong learning. It is in the interest of all of us to restore the classical model of education.

Shifting our educational paradigm from factory techniques that view education as producing humans fit for the economics of mass production back to the ideal that education prepares mankind for freedom is hard to do while also trying to shift the responsibility of educating children from professionals back to the family. Separately, these ideas are difficult enough to implement. Embracing home-centered education and classical education at the same time seems impossible; yet millions of families are managing to do so. C. S. Lewis, the author of *The Chronicles of Narnia,* said, "The only people who achieve much are those who want knowledge so badly that they seek it while the conditions are still unfavourable. Favourable conditions never come." Let's seek to improve our children's education in spite of the difficulties. Many of the ideas in this book are just commonsense things you do anyway with your family. Studying with a greater purpose may motivate you to become more intentional in raising children who love to learn.

One of the challenges of home-centered education is building a new relationship with your children. If you decide to become more involved in your children's education, you may be worried about how to assume the new role of your child's instructor. You might be used to being a nurturing disciplinarian and providing leadership in your home, but fear that becoming your child's teacher is altogether different.

In order to teach your children classically, you may have to teach them to respect you in a different way, and you may have to become worthy of their respect. Adding the role of teacher to your parental repertoire can be done, however, and may lead to wonderful developments in your family. Contrary to popular culture, it is natural for children to recognize that parents are wiser than themselves and for young adults to want to be personally responsible. Let's resolve to be adults whom children like to spend time with, not because we are "fun," but because our kids know that we think it is a great privilege and pleasure to be with them. Let's show them that when we learn something new, we can't wait to share our discovery with them. Where there is a vision, parents will find a way.

My sons know that the following is their parents' vision for their academic education as children. The vision can only mature as they become young men if the core is solid and the foundations are steady.

My belief is that studying the classics makes us well-rounded and instills in us a sense and appreciation of the world in a unique way. In the following chapters, I give readers the tools to tackle any subject. A key aspect of my methodology is treating the particulars of any subject as a core set of ideas, called grammar (that is, the rudiments, or basic elements). The grammatical concepts chosen for this book are based on the experience of a group of families who worked together to develop a rigorous, classical education for their high school students. Both the adults and students recognized they were lacking some core ideas that could have been studied at a much earlier age. Our lack of knowledge was only slowing us down at higher levels of learning. As the leader of the families, I was determined that our younger children should not miss out on such obviously important information. This curriculum has now been used by tens of thousands of families through the organization of academic communities I founded called Classical Conversations.

The final chapter offers some schedules and tips for implementing the classical model no matter where your children attend school. Everyone says parents are children's first and best teachers. I really believe it.

As a minimum before high school, my children should be able to:

- Read and discuss newspaper articles, the Bible, winners of the Newbery Medal for children's literature, as well as the content of magazines such as *Popular Mechanics*.

Diverse reading opportunities, from current events, science magazines, and great literature along with the comics in the Sunday paper broaden students' vocabulary. Details are explained in Chapter Four, "Reading."

- Diagram sentences while identifying the 4 structures, the 4 purposes, and the 7 patterns of a sentence, the 8 parts of speech, and any additional clauses or phrases in at least two languages. Write a keyword outline from multiple sources and synthesize into a single short essay.

By working on one sentence a day for six years for 180 school days, a student can exhaustively parse 1,080 sentences in elementary school. The structure of writing should be emphasized over the creative content. Details are explained in Chapter Five, "Writing."

- Be able to quickly multiply and divide through the 15 × 15 table, memorize the common squares and cubes, identify the associative, commutative, distributive, and identity laws in math problems, add and subtract multiple digits in their heads, and have mastered basic forms of numbers.

There are many other concepts they should master such as shapes, patterns, using our decimal system, and measurement. The ideas listed above are the most important concepts, though by no means exhaustive. However, the concepts most needed are also the most often neglected, as explained in Chapter Six, "Math." No calculators should be needed until trigonometry is studied in mid-high school.

- Draw a map of the world and label two hundred locations from memory.

This has proven to be very easy for children if they are encouraged to draw from the time they can hold a crayon, as this provides much practice in sitting still and copying. Details are explained in Chapter Seven, "Geography."

- List a time line that includes 160 world events and the 44 U.S. presidents from memory.

By memorizing 8 events a week, it takes about 25 weeks to memorize the time line. Then students should recite 32 to 40 events a day until the time line is internalized. Details are explained in Chapter Eight, "History."

- Be able to identify basic science categories and memorize key ideas from each category.

The basic science of the universe is framed through five main categories: astronomy, the earth sciences, biology, chemistry, and physics. G. K. Chesterton said, "We perish from want of wonder, not from want of wonders." Children should go outside, be shown how to open their eyes and wonder at the marvels of creation. As adults teach children to name the animals, plants, constellations, and processes they observe, they should also show them how the brain can systematically file these ideas for comparison and contrast. Details are explained in Chapter Nine, "Science."

- Be able to control their bodies for extended periods of time, whether they're bored or not. Be able to participate in sports, draw, and play an instrument. Be able to identify masters of fine arts including composers, painters, and even athletes.

Fine arts should never be thought of as egalitarian any more than any other field of study. Those who create and preserve "high culture" in the arts help those of us who admire beauty to understand that, by comparison, "pop culture" is the equivalent of a diet of potato chips and candy. Enjoying classical culture requires more effort, but once understanding is reached, we are forever hungry for more. Details are explained in Chapter Ten, "Fine Arts."

PART ONE

———

THE CLASSICAL MODEL

CHAPTER ONE

WHAT'S WRONG WITH EDUCATION TODAY?

"If you approve, headmaster, I will stay as I am here as long as any boy wants to read the classics. I think it would be very wicked indeed to do anything to fit a boy for the modern world."

"It's a short-sided view, Scott-King."

"There, headmaster, with all respect, I differ from you profoundly. I think it the most long-sighted view it is possible to take."

—*Evelyn Waugh*, "Scott-King's Modern Europe"

THE PURPOSE OF CLASSICAL EDUCATION

There are many practical purposes for schooling: vocational skills, hobbies, earning a living, social interaction, or just enlarging perspectives. The purpose of a classical education is to equip students to discover the way our universe works. Understanding the physical universe requires a foundational knowledge of math and science. Understanding human nature requires a foundational knowledge of language, history, economics, and literature. To learn foundational information from any field of knowledge, students need to be trained in reading, writing, communication, and analysis of qualitative information. At their highest level, the humanities are studied because they embody the ideas that make us human.

We exchange knowledge, information, and ideas through words, spoken or symbolic. Words are processed, weighed, and analyzed through other words, even if they originated in a picture or image or experience. Words are used to share concrete and abstract ideas. Words allow us to build great cities, negotiate peace between countries, and share a pleasant meal with friends and family. The goal of education is to teach children to become adults who can handle complex ideas, in uncertain situations, with confidence. We feel confident when we can competently manage words and ideas.

Successful education ought to propel a student to want to learn more. Learning should inspire joy bound with constant astonishment at the marvels of creation. Learning should breathe life into us—ignite our imaginations and inspire us to share the ideas we learn with people we love. The joy of learning begins in the home, with the entire world as our classroom. I believe children learn best when their parents and teachers are their heroes.

Classical education consists of teaching the skills of grammar, logic (also called dialectic), and rhetoric. These skills are called the trivium, which is Latin for "three roads," or a place where three ways meet. In the Middle Ages, the trivium was the lower division of the seven liberal arts, before the quadrivium. (More about that in Chapter Six.) Although modern education purports to teach the liberal arts, it has unknowingly neglected the benefits of the various classical arts that form a good education, especially its rigors.

The foundation of a classical education begins with parents teaching children the art of memorization and grammar studies. Some educators might dismiss rote memorization, but I argue that it is beneficial because it trains your brain to hold information. It is the most organic way of learning ever devised and goes hand in hand with the way we naturally relate to our children.

This is a process that starts at the beginning. From the moment that parents hold their baby in their arms a bonding process begins. They talk to the child; they introduce the sounds and names of the world around them to the baby through repetition. ("Look at the puppy. See the puppy?") The mother and father of a newborn find no hardship in saying words like "I love you," or "Yes, I'm your mommy," in patient intonations over and over, a thousand times. By doing so, the baby begins to identify big ideas like warmth, hunger, kindness, and dinner with specific words and actions, thus developing a vocabulary. Many pediatricians agree that the best thing for a child's neurological development is for parents to engage the child's mind by using a multitude of words and touches. Yet somehow, in recent years educational theory has come to reject repetition as a good educational tool when it comes to mastering our multiplication tables or identifying geographic locations or learning the correct spelling of words. We accept that to be good at sports or music you must practice over and over until your fine motor skills become your gross motor skills, meaning that you can play Tchaikovsky in your sleep! Over-practice implies enough repetition to make new skills seem easy and natural. Yet contemporary educational philosophies consider large amounts of rote practice to be unnecessary in academics. And so our modern educational system is weak.

The purpose of a classical education is to strengthen one's mind, body, and character in order to develop the ability to learn anything. This requires consistent discipleship or mentoring by a concerned adult over a long period of time with very specific academic goals. For eventually, the child wants to know why she must learn so much terminology and what to do with what she has learned. These natural questions lead children into dialectic and rhetorical studies.

Before we examine the restoration of the classical model as the core for every child's education, let's explore the ideology that caused us to lose the classical model after 2,500 years of success. The main culprits that have reduced our ability to engage in reasonable discourse are professionalism, federal mandates, "edutainment," and the desertion of memorization skills.

PROFESSIONALISM REPLACES PARENTING

Specialization and division of labor are hallmarks of professionalism in any field. Just like doctors and lawyers, modern educators mimic the efficiencies of the assembly line by specializing in a very particular field such as fourth-grade science or pre-reading development. Specialization may be helpful in teaching adults who want to learn a specific skill and it can be very helpful for overcoming a particular learning disability, but it is not particularly helpful in fostering a love for learning in children who are just trying to please their teacher so they can get back to the important business of playing with their toys.

Schooling is now equally professionalized. Instead of parents who guide their children through home, community, and work life, we now assign students to professional educators charged with teaching each child a specialty for an hour a day for fifteen weeks, and then the students move on to a new subject led by a different teacher. Students have no time to bond with their mentor or to discover and appreciate the wisdom of their instructor. Students are given no opportunity to watch their instructor struggle with learning, to copy the teacher's perseverance and character, to see over the course of time that their mentors continue their studies as an ongoing pursuit. Children are designed to be nurtured, taught, and loved by two adults within a supportive community for an extended period of time. Instead, we put children in a situation where they are consistently molded to depend on their peers. Children are taught to value the other students more than their teachers, for at least their classmates follow them on the age-graded conveyor belt from class to class, year after year, whereas teachers come and go.

As we leave the industrial age, the new age of global technologies requires parents and teachers to examine our current educational structures. The government has funded many initiatives and innovations in an attempt to repair modern education. They all fail, however, because they forget that children need consistent, ongoing guidance from someone they trust.

Helping small children who live in the worst circumstances is one reason most of us justify professionalized education. Yet the structure we have built to protect and nurture these children actually does the opposite. Imagine an impoverished six-year-old boy who rarely gets a healthy meal and rarely has parental supervision. He finally goes to school and falls in love with the first person who has ever been there every day for him—his first-grade teacher. She loves and encourages and teaches him. She won't let the kids bully one another, and she makes sure he gets a good breakfast, lunch, and an after-school snack. Only the weekends are scary. The six-year-old has a daily routine that includes a committed relationship for the very first time. Life is good; hope is learned. Then the school year ends, and this wonderful teacher says, "Good-bye. You will have a great teacher in second grade."

So the seven-year-old survives the short summer and begins the process all over. But now he has a homeroom teacher, a math and science teacher, a language arts teacher, and a music teacher. Which one is he to fall in love with? Who will fall in love with him? Each of these teachers has dozens of students to care for an hour at a time. And so, at the end of second grade it's a little less painful to part with his teachers because he never really got to know them. But at least he was physically safe and was fed every day.

And so, by the end of third grade, he hardly notices his teacher because he has formed a strong attachment to the friends who move along from class to class with him. They share multiple hours together daily.

Instead of taking his signals of proper behavior from a committed adult, since he has none at home or school, he models his life after the future football captain, just as the girls in his class likely emulate the future prom queen. This child from an impoverished culture was taught, in effect, that no adult cares enough to hang out and teach him for more than the 150 hours required to complete a credit. And as he got older, he also learned that the teachers were not quite as able to physically protect him as when he and his classmates were small, and it's humiliating to have to eat the government-provided free lunch.

Even our elementary schools offer fewer and fewer years of a single teacher leading a class of students through all of the subjects. We've hired professionals and experts to separate the subjects as though humans can segment their lives into artificial compartments. Then the adults wonder why the skills children learned in one "unit" of the day don't translate into another. By our methods of presentation we have taught them to think that they are unrelated. The focus now is on course content and professionalization rather than on the nature of educating a whole, young person who can only become a mature adult by spending time with other mature adults.

The factory has produced the product we asked for—a student who exists in the system and gets by until he is released from compulsory education. No adult committed to understanding the questions burning in his heart, and besides, the Discovery Channel presentations were more interesting than the substitute teacher. Through our good intentions, we offered this needy student a system that ignored him—a child created to work hard and feel the satisfying encouragement of a loving adult while conquering difficult challenges. We offered him a system that kept him occupied but did not endow him with the abilities to continue his studies independently.

I am criticizing the professionalization of teaching children because these young human beings are not cogs in a machine. And I am trying to identify the root of the problem for all those wonderful adults who went into teaching thinking that they could commit to nurturing the lives of many children only to end up having the system squash their excellent motives. Our current school system replicates factories and requires classroom managers more than teachers. Teachers are appreciably frustrated.

Besides teaching children to love learning, it is important to teach children to respect their family. I am a paid teacher, but I know that any time I do something to break the bond between a student and a parent, I weaken that family. Families rely on one another for a lifetime, whereas I am only with them for a season. I want my students to spend as much time as possible with their parents and siblings, while learning to respect the difficulties experienced by the other members of the family. I want to turn my students' attentions to their parents' values. I want my students to know that their parents are smart; that children can trust their parents to help them with academic difficulties. I want discussions on difficult issues within the classroom to be frank and honest while I am tutoring, but I want to end every conversation with, "Now go home and ask your parents what they think." Families are designed to nurture the minds, wills, and emotions of its members so that the barriers created by fear of the unknown can be replaced by the confidence that comes from knowing you are loved whether you succeed or fail.

Whether the student from previous American generations lived with a concerned parent or in a neglectful situation, our citizens universally experienced a much higher level of reading comprehension compared to today's students. Professionalized instruction has resulted in a large loss of literacy for both strong and dysfunctional families. In contrast, consider how successful one-room, community schoolhouses used to be. Our country had proficient literacy rates of over 90 percent when first-grade children were in the same room as seventh-graders and children attended school for just a few months a year. Someone who has acquired proficient levels of literacy can analyze and synthesize a variety of ideas from a wide range of documents and defend her conclusions by using the source text. This is a much higher, nimbler level of literacy than just being able to read a novel or newspaper.

A large percentage of American colonists purchased documents that required the ability to read proficiently. French political thinker and historian Alexis de Tocqueville commented on how everyone in America read all kinds of treaties, unlike the Europeans he studied. For the first three hundred years after colonists first settled here, American parents taught children how to read and work and think. Why were the parents able to teach their children? They just taught what they had been taught when they were young. If you know how to add, subtract, multiply, and divide, you can certainly teach a child math. If you know how to read, you can help a nonreading child become a reader. It is just common sense. But nowadays parents are led to believe that only professionals in a classroom situation know how to properly teach children.

FEDERAL MANDATES REPLACED COMMUNITY AND HOME SCHOOLS

We live in a society that believes it is the federal government's job to provide education for the masses, from daycare through college and beyond, including classes for senior citizens. Until professionals replaced the parent as the chief educator of children, federal mandates removed control from the community, and entertainment replaced hard work as the model of education. (Before the 1950s, there were no elementary schools. Instead, they were called grammar schools because that is what everyone knew children should study.)

Now we are a nation of parents who believe that if our children don't *enjoy* school, something must be wrong with the books or the teacher, but not with the children. Or we seek special labels to justify our children's weaknesses so they can be given individual instruction that then tries to replicate the very family life we have removed them from. Psychologists and counselors are employed to provide a firm, nurturing, parental hand for struggling children because their parents have been told they are unqualified to fulfill this role.

Curriculum providers, too, are happy to perpetuate the illusion that if we could just find the "magic recipe," our children could learn without requiring intense struggle and difficulty. Likewise, publishers are delighted to sell new editions that claim to have the newest, quickest, most "fun" child-led techniques.

But, realistically, academic excellence occurs only when one thing happens: everyone works hard whether they want to or not, and whether they are good at it or not. As the parents of four children, my husband and I have heard every excuse about why they don't want to study. As a teacher and educational advisor, I've heard every possible excuse from parents about why their child can't perform or doesn't enjoy certain aspects of learning.

Parents have forgotten that a century ago, the average nine-year-old worked hard enough to earn his or her own way in life. I wish every child had a life so blessed with ease that he thought loading the dishes into a dishwasher was hard work, but that is not reality. Parents need to stop believing excuses from poor Johnny that learning is too hard, or that he can't pay attention, or that practicing penmanship is boring, or that math is repetitive. Tough. Life is repetitive. We are crippling our children's brains instead of providing the extensive mental exercise they need for normal development. Mental exercise with a core of quality material is comparable to physical exercise with a healthy diet. It would be interesting to study whether our academic decline has paralleled our increased obesity as a nation.

It is time to restore the academic levels achieved by all schoolchildren in the United States before the 1950s when *proficient* literacy was universally expected as evidenced by the numbers of books purchased, the extensive vocabulary used in children's literature, and the number of complex ideas connected in a single, lengthy sentence. People write as they think and speak. The popular writers of even the recent past like Thoreau, Alcott, and Douglas, are difficult to read by those of us taught to think in tweets. America is a global leader, and to continue to compete around the world, we have to start working as hard at learning as our friends in India and China. If we do not, we will have no right to complain about jobs or political power going overseas. The U.S. will regain academic leadership if we restore the classical model as an educational ideal and restore the belief that parents are smart enough to be in charge of their children's education.

We need to reintroduce families to American heroes who have overcome real educational handicaps (not mere inconvenience) to achieve academic excellence. One of my heroes is Helen Keller. Though blind and deaf, Helen became an international figure before the age of radio or movies. Most of us are familiar with "Teacher," Annie Sullivan, from the biographical movie *The Miracle Worker*. Annie was a true teacher in that she made Helen do hard things and overcome many disabilities.

I am in awe of the imagination and determination this deaf and blind woman possessed in order to achieve what she did. She could "hear" a radio by touching the radio and feeling the vibrations! But I am even more deeply moved by her joy for life in spite of living in total darkness. In her 1951 biography of Helen Keller titled *Journey into Light*, Ishbel Ross says, "She found Franklin D. Roosevelt an ideal subject [for lip reading by vibration]. She caught Mark Twain's best jokes by vibration. With her fingers on his lips Enrico Caruso 'poured his golden voice' into her hand. Feodor Chaliapin shouted the 'Song of Volga Boatman' with his arm encircling her tightly so that she could feel every vibration of his mighty voice. Jascha Heifetz played for her while her fingers rested lightly on his violin. She read Carl Sandburg's verses from his lips and old plantation folk songs from the rim of his guitar."

Most people today won't even recognize the names of these internationally historic treasures, let alone think it is important to introduce these artists' contributions to our "healthy" children, possessed with full faculties, who could easily appreciate the classical arts in comparison to Helen. Though blind, Helen Keller was such a voracious reader that as she felt the words in braille her fingers bled and needed to be wrapped in silk so that she could read more. We must be willing to foster diligence in our children. Annie worked methodically for hours with young Helen, often at great personal cost, until Helen gained enough self-control to become teachable. When my children say they are tired of studying, I ask, "Are your fingers bleeding from writing so much?" Since they know Helen's story, they respond with, "No, but my hand is cramping!" I believe parents love their children even more than Annie loved Helen.

We parents also have to deal with the entertainment society engulfing us. Parents even say they would die *for* one of their children, yet somehow they find it difficult to live *with* them. I initially found it hard to be a parent, especially when I knew I could be paid to do things I liked equally well. When I became a mother, no one told me it would take about three years to figure things out. I had always worked or been in school. I had to only be responsible for myself. Now there were babies who couldn't talk demanding my attention. I had to learn how to enjoy being a parent.

Now I love it. We read, work on math problems, do chores, and play together. We also fight and sometimes make each other cry. There are times when I'd like to send my children away to boarding school and other times when I wish I had more children. I like the way that I have a different bond with each son. One talks business and politics with me. One remodels with me. One shares my appreciation of computers. One wants me to help him share his Christian faith with his neighborhood friends. For me, the things that seem natural are the things that seem familiar. The root of the words "familiar" and "family" are the same, the Latin *familia,* "household." It is natural to want to be with your family. They are the ones who will encourage hard work, rejoicing over successes and empathizing with difficulties.

DESERTION OF MEMORIZATION SKILLS

Comedian Jay Leno regularly mocks our educational system through his "Jay Walking" segments on *The Tonight Show.* We groan and laugh and shake our heads and then confirm his proposition that we are a nation of dunces by waiting for him to crack the next joke instead of turning off the TV and cracking a book. We want the impossible—a better education by being entertained.

Before the 1950s, one of the ways students were tested on their core knowledge was through recitations. They might recite a long poem like Longfellow's *Hiawatha* for literature, orally parse a compound-complex sentence, list a history timeline, chant a multiplication table, or sketch a continent and its main features. Students were expected to do this with just their brain as a reference tool. Somewhere along the way, professional education associations decided that facts could be looked up, and so there was no point in memorizing them. Critical thinking skills and experiential learning replaced memorization as the main focus of grammar school instruction.

Though critical thinking skills and experiential learning are very valuable, the education associations forgot two things: first, that students needed to memorize information so they would have something in their brain to critically think about or to compare to their experiences, and, second, that the brain needs to be intentionally trained in order to think well. Thinking critically is not inherent in humans. It needs to be practiced repeatedly by comparing memorized ideas with new ideas in a logical manner. Internalizing a critical mass of words and ideas is the first step to thinking well.

For example, we naturally speak English if we grow up around English-speaking people. Even without instruction, young children have memorized so much of the patterns of their mother tongue that they can recognize an error in speech and correct it. The focus of grammar school should be memorization of the rules of grammar for reading, writing, and arithmetic in order to facilitate clear reasoning so that the maturing student can recognize and correct errors on his own.

Today's schools have replaced memorization skills in elementary education with fun activities and have pushed memorization into high school subjects. We expect high school students to memorize many new terms from different subject areas, yet we have never helped them develop a method. For example, learning the taxonomies of species, the periodic table, and foreign languages all require the memorization of long lists of words. But because the neglect of grammar memorization causes high school students to struggle to reproduce the information studied in a semester on a final exam, we have regressed, or devolved, to multiple-choice tests that provide lots of visual clues so that if they at least paid some attention to the subject, they can guess the correct answer. In fact, we now offer courses that teach high school students *how to guess* on their standardized college boards so they can score higher. Too bad they aren't offered a course on memorization instead.

Speaking of tests, I am a big fan of testing, if testing is a quick way for a student to assess where he or she needs to spend more time studying. Instead tests are used to determine, well . . . I don't know what tests are used for anymore because we move students to the next grade and the next teacher no matter what the test results indicate. The general student and parent population seem to assume that tests are relevant only to teachers, when really they should predominately be for the students' use. Tests should be a valuable opportunity for self-evaluation and feedback from a trusted adult.

REDUCED ABILITY TO READ PROFICIENTLY

One of the ideals of classical education is preparation for civic involvement. Whether reciting one of Cicero's addresses to the Roman senate or the Mayflower Compact, since the early 1600s schoolchildren in America were expected to memorize and effectively deliver influential political statements in order to ensure they understood the role of a citizen. In the United States, we have documents our Founding Fathers wrote in order to outline the basic tenets by which we Americans have agreed to live. Parents are often stunned at the high level of literacy required to read and understand these important documents. Studies have shown that these foundational documents are unfamiliar to most of our citizens. We can only be complacent, passive citizens if we are unable to comprehend the expansive vocabulary of our nation's founders and can't explain the laws governing our country.

Neil Postman, in his book *Amusing Ourselves to Death,* explains how the age of show business has nullified book banning because no one bothers to even read. He believed that our love for the "technologies that undo our capacity to think" would make us into a culture that would lose its appetite for books and subsequently its ability to process difficult ideas or large quantities of information. In 1985, he predicted our severe reduction in literary skills, since he foresaw popular entertainment replacing attendance at lectures and symposiums.

America's schools are no longer inculcating the love of great thoughts because everyone seems confused about the true nature of education, and about who bears the responsibility for educating children—is it the school or the parents? According to Peter F. Drucker in his book *Post-Capitalist Society,* schools fail to teach literacy because they are being asked to do impossible tasks, such as to socialize students. Family, places of worship, and communities are designed for socializing. According to Drucker, schools should not be expected to replace the family or house of worship or community center. Typical annual school board reports often emphasize core values such as diversity, empathy, equality, innovativeness, and integrity over core skills such as reading, writing, and arithmetic.

LITERACY STATISTICS AND DEFINITIONS

According to both the National Assessment of Educational Progress (NAEP) and National Association of Adult Literacy (NAAL), our adult American population had only a 15 percent rate of literacy proficiency in 2007. Today, policymakers distinguish between several types of literacy. There are three basic categories of literacy: prose, document, and quantitative. Prose literacy refers to the ability to search, comprehend, and use continuous texts such as brochures, newspaper or magazine articles, books, and instructions. Document literacy refers to the ability to comprehend noncontinuous texts such as job applications, payroll schedules, maps, and graphs. Quantitative literacy refers to the ability to identify and perform computations using numbers embedded in print, as in balancing a checkbook, calculating tips, and using order forms.

In 2005, based on statistics from 2003, the National Assessment of Adult Literacy estimated that 13 percent of Americans are proficient (able to use complex and challenging texts) in prose literacy. Forty-four percent were at the intermediate level (handling moderately challenging texts), 29 percent were basic (handling simple and everyday tasks), and 14 percent were below basic (comprehending only simple and concrete texts).

The same study found that in the category of document literacy, 13 percent were proficient, 53 percent were intermediate, 22 percent were basic, and 12 percent were below basic. In quantitative literacy, 13 percent were proficient, 33 percent were intermediate, 33 percent were basic, and 22 percent were below basic.

In general, the U.S. Department of Education distinguishes between functional literacy and literacy, and also between literacy and English literacy. The NAAL estimates that 11 million adults sixteen and over are not literate in English, and were not calculated in the general literacy statistics.

I give these numbers and examples to dispel the misconception that today's Americans are better educated than previous generations. It's just not true that more years of compulsory school attendance have translated to a more educated populace. Did you pay attention to the NAAL stats? Only about *13 percent* of American adults were proficient readers from 2003 to 2007.

Because most American adults struggle with reading difficult material, it is not surprising that our high school students are also struggling. Free education has proven to be the same as a free lunch: there just "ain't" no such thing. During a course I took for my postgraduate studies, one of my professors from the school's education department suggested, "Schools are our most educationally impoverished institutions."

Many parents may dismiss my message because their kids are getting As, enjoy going to school, and are learning basic skills like multiplication. In general, parents acknowledge that modern education is in crisis, but few believe that *their* children attend a school with real problems. My response is that our standards of even basic literacy are too low. I had one parent email me that I was lying when I said schools no longer taught the multiplication tables. I responded that I'm sure some are teaching the multiplication tables, but I doubted any were teaching them through 20 × 20 or making the students memorize fractional tables. It's not that teachers aren't trying; it's that the standards aren't rigorous.

If you disagree with me, please read the following paragraph from Thomas Paine's widely read pamphlet, *Common Sense,* which advocated colonial America's independence from England.

Thus necessity, like a gravitating power, would soon form our newly arrived emigrants into society, the reciprocal blessings of which would supersede, and render the obligations of law and government unnecessary while they remained perfectly just to each other; but as nothing but Heaven is impregnable to vice, it will unavoidably happen that in proportion as they surmount the first difficulties of emigration, which bound them together in a common cause, they will begin to relax in their duty and attachment to each other: and this remissness will point out the necessity of establishing some form of government to supply the defect of moral virtue.

This pamphlet was written to be read by the average teenager in 1776. Few modern adults, let alone high school students, can read this document well enough to explain its arguments and conclusions. Parents need to recognize that our current literacy and numeracy standards are far below our children's abilities. A study conducted in 1800 by Du Pont de Nemours revealed that only four in a thousand Americans were unable to read and write legibly. Various accounts from colonial America support these statistics. In 1772 Jacob Duché, the chaplain of the Continental Congress (who later turned Tory), wrote:

> The poorest labourer upon the shore of Delaware thinks himself entitled to deliver his sentiments in matters of religion or politics with as much freedom as the gentleman or scholar. . . . Such is the prevailing taste for books of every kind, that almost every man is a reader; and by pronouncing sentence, right or wrong, upon the various publications that come in his way, puts himself upon a level, in point of knowledge, with their several authors.

Even those who rarely attended school in the colonies could read better than we have been led to believe. Overall, the same percentage of Americans read *Common Sense* in the late 1770s that watch the Super Bowl today! Can we name a political document that everyone is reading today? The news is full of people commenting on and congressmen voting on important documents that, sometimes by their own admission, they haven't actually read. According to our own department of education, only 15 percent of our adult populace is proficient in reading.

PERCENTAGE OF ADULTS PROFICIENT IN READING PROSE, BY GENDER		
	1992	2003
Female	14%	14%
Male	16%	13%
Both	15%	13%
Source: U.S. Department of Education, National Center for Education Statistics		

A gentleman at my gym approached me one day and said, "Do you know how we make fun of the employees at McDonald's because they don't know how to make change without the register telling them what to do? Well, my daughter just got a job running a cash register. She came home crying from work the first day because she realized she doesn't know how to make change. She is a straight-A senior at the local high school. How did this happen?" We had never spoken before and he had no idea who I was. He told me his children went to an elite, private school in the Bahamas until they attended their local high school in the United States. This caring, engaged father discovered that getting good grades in school no longer means a child is educated. He voiced regret that he and his wife had trusted the school system—both public and private—and we discussed how too often an A means the student behaved and was pleasant to the teacher.

THE STATE OF EDUCATION IN THE UNITED STATES
According to the government's own statistics . . .

- In 2004, China graduated 500,000 engineers, and India graduated 200,000 engineers, while the United States graduated only 70,000 engineers.
- Until the 1950s education cost practically nothing; and the United States had a literacy rate of 90 percent or better. Today, the District of Columbia spends over $13,000 a year per student; and . . .
- Less than 50 percent of American high school students graduate as proficient readers.
- Less than 15 percent of American high school students graduate as proficient mathematicians.
- In 2006, only 60 percent of high school seniors graduated.

SURVEYING TEXTBOOKS REPLACED STUDYING ORIGINAL DOCUMENTS

Modern education depends on textbooks. Instead, teachers should demand that our older students struggle with difficult arguments from a wide range of original documents and great literary works. The author or team of authors of a textbook have sorted through standard references and consulted educational associations to determine what basic information should be included in their volume. The authors and editors do the hard work of summarizing the most important information relating to a subject instead of letting students research and summarize the information. Today's high school students, far from expecting to write papers daily, groan when they hear that a single paper will be required of them.

Textbooks can be great reference tools when a student is researching an unfamiliar topic, but most students never fully engage with a topic if they use only textbooks. All the interesting questions have already been asked and answered for the student by someone else. These days it is rare for a student to identify a textbook that was formative in developing great habits of research, reading, and recitation. Textbooks are structured differently than they were before the 1950s. A well-organized textbook can show students how to determine their own outline for a systematic study of a subject, but contemporary textbooks are not used in that way. Today texts are like nannies, holding your hand each step of the way—as though the authors think they have to tell the student and teacher what to do on Mondays at 9:37 A.M.—rather than as a point to begin more intensive studies. The proliferation of textbooks in schools is testimony to the misguided belief that children are unwilling to struggle with ideas and want all their work done for them and placed in a single source.

Today's schools also use a different textbook each year for a different subject. This appeases our desire for everything to be new in order to seem like it is the best. The fact that this is a recent phenomena is illustrated by the sales of McGuffey (also McGuffey's) Readers and Noah Webster's "Blue-Backed Spellers." They were used for many grade levels and for many generations. Now texts come and go quicker than such fads as pet rocks, or the latest model of iPod.

In the 1990s, I was expressing my delight in discovering the use of objective complements to a pair of retired English teachers when they both blurted out in unison, "Warriner's Grammar, page 33." These two women taught in two completely different school systems in two different eras, yet both had used the same text, John E. Warriner's *English Grammar and Composition,* in college and in their classroom. They knew the key grammar to teach because they had been taught the same core. (For additional evidence of the change in educational emphasis, Warriner's later editions reversed the title to *English Composition and Grammar.* The grammar was moved to the back of the book from the front as if grammar is an afterthought rather than foundational to compostion.) Before the printing press, one was defined as educated if one had memorized large quantities of information. Relying on books has actually robbed us of the opportunity to naturally exercise our minds through recitations. Now videos are deteriorating our reading proficiency and are rapidly reducing our common vocabulary. Texting has reduced us even further to just grunting at one another through consonants. Tweets have made our speech quick yet ugly.

The classically educated student learns how to use all the methods of communication mentioned above rather than abandoning the tried and true for the trendy. A student who reads Shakespeare's plays is able to appreciate a movie far more than the student who abandons her computer screen to sit in front of a movie screen. But a student who *memorizes* soliloquies and other passages from Shakespeare's plays can enjoy a movie far more than the one who only reads Shakespeare, for she brings Shakespeare's thoughts into the movie theater with her. She can evaluate the movie's themes in light of not only the movie director's images and her own experience but also the ideas of a dramatist from another century, composed in language rich with puns, irony, allusions to myth and history, "and much more."

REDUCTION OF REASONABLE DISCOURSE

When I began teaching my children, I realized that even though the world said I was educated, I found out I was only schooled. My husband, whom

I met at the University of Michigan, was returning for his third degree, this time in aerospace engineering, after having earned degrees in music and natural resources. He couldn't believe how ill-prepared his classmates were compared to his peers from a previous decade. I had to work hard, but he just worked smart. It turned out that he had received a classical education from the homework his European parents insisted he do when the school neglected to send any home. It took me two years of mediocre grades and a lot of tutoring in college before I realized that there was an art to studying.

I completed my degree with a decent GPA due to grade inflation, yet I couldn't comprehend the French in *Henry V,* the Latin phrases in the *National Review* magazine, or the English in *The Federalist Papers.* I couldn't tell you a single constellation, the name of an African country or an Australian province. I could not say what century Charles Martel, Pepin the Short, and Charlemagne lived in, whether they were related to one another, or what kingdoms they ruled. I could read very quickly, but to this day my vocabulary is limited. I knew a major change was needed in our family's educational approach when I had difficulty in explaining to my son why he should write "should've" rather than "should of." I knew "should of" was grammatically wrong, but didn't know enough about the parts of speech to explain why.

I struggled in college because I had never been asked to work hard in high school. Why had no one demanded that I read difficult material so I could improve my vocabulary? Why had no one demonstrated the art of recitation? Why had no teacher asked me to synthesize my learning experiences in the context of world history or pursue the great questions and mysteries of mankind? Reading graded, compartmentalized, abridged information for a semester, then answering basic reading comprehension questions on multiple choice exams allowed one to pass through high school. Getting through seemed to be the object.

Education is supposed to prepare children for adulthood. Adults are expected to be able to understand basic math and the stock market so they can buy groceries and have savings when they are old, grasp basic chemistry and biology so they can make healthy eating choices, vote intelligently for leaders who will preserve our freedoms, grapple with the ethical issues associated with advancing technologies, and navigate a global marketplace that is becoming increasingly smaller. Adults need to be able to discuss these significant topics with local merchants, neighbors, and colleagues so we can all make more informed decisions.

If I am not able to read, write, and reflect on issues that define citizenship, how can I teach my children to do so? By not teaching our children the art of learning, we are raising a culture that is unable to engage in reasonable discourse. As the world gets smaller and smaller, we will need to preserve our most noble American qualities as they mingle with ideas and customs from other parts of the world. This requires a citizenry that can step back from the daily strain of living and examine life in a larger perspective. We can assess and act upon lessons learned from the downfall of Rome or the persecution of the Sudanese or the building of the Berlin Wall without having personally lived through them. It also requires a citizenry that can intellectually engage the parliaments of the world, as did antislavery advocate William Wilberforce or Benjamin Franklin, and sacrifice personal power, as did Washington or Gandhi.

Ravi Zacharias, a popular debater at Ivy League schools, challenges us to think about how we value words.

We are living in a time when sensitivities are at the surface, often vented with cutting words. Philosophically, you can believe anything, so long as you do not claim it to be true. Morally, you can practice anything, so long as you do not claim that it is a "better" way.

A classicalist believes words have meanings and that semantics matter. If a word's meaning changes within every context, communication can't occur, as I can never be sure that you meant what you said. It requires diligence to craft a well-written statement and it would be hardly worth the effort if the words you used were never taken in context or treated as though you really didn't believe what you said. I am proposing that the classical model is a better way of education because I believe that words can express enduring truth, goodness, and beauty as real and measurable as the words of Moses, Aristotle, and Aquinas.

REJECTION OF GREAT CLASSICAL CONVERSATIONS

Because our educational system has rejected many of the traditional tools of learning, we can no longer participate in the great classical conversations of history. We no longer have the ability to make use of the wisdom of the great thinkers from other eras and other continents. My local elementary school's billboard recently proclaimed the slogan, "We are teaching children for the future, not for the past." Either it was stating something ridiculously obvious or it was announcing the principal's intention to dismiss the past as irrelevant to the future. It was a characteristically contemporary thought, especially given that the past is really the only thing we can study. It is impossible to study the future, and the present becomes the past pretty quickly.

We need to offer our children the past as an important measure of their future. I don't want my children ever to think that fascism or totalitarianism are great new ideas. It used to be that when evil came around again, it would disguise itself with a new name. Will our children be so ignorant of the past that evil will no longer have to be clever to fool them? The past is very important to their future. In logic, a chronological fallacy is to think that just because something is old, it is useless. Instead, it could be truly timeless.

Since the time of Socrates, Plato, and Aristotle, teachers believed the purpose of education was to pursue truth, goodness, and beauty and to develop wisdom and virtue. Classical academies in Alexandria and Jerusalem, the monasteries of the Roman Catholic Church in Europe, and the Protestant seminaries in America all shared this pursuit by preserving and studying the great works of literature from a wide variety of cultures and philosophies. Historically, teachers thought it was important to share the collective knowledge of the ages through various forms of schools and to synthesize the ideals of the ancients with contemporaries and the discoveries of the East with the West.

The school in third-century Alexandria began to formalize the academic processes or skills of grammar (recitation and memorization), dialectic (discussions with the purpose to discern truth), and rhetoric (the ability to take the grammar understood and teach it to others). Until the modern era, a single teacher would take a handful of youths and spend the time needed to develop a deep relationship through the pursuit of academics. The tutor would continue the discipleship the students' parents had begun. Students from the early academies wrote about loving instructors such as the early Christian theologian Origen. In the fourth century, Augustine helped to establish education as an important duty of the church. The cathedral schools of Charlemagne's time and later emphasized order and a desire to foster universal literacy.

In the twelfth century, some teachers began to establish Western universities apart from the monasteries, but they still emphasized character and culture. During the Reformation, man began to believe he could learn about nature and nature's God without depending on his priest. Erasmus, Luther, and Calvin emphasized both the teaching of doctrine and educational methods. Francis Bacon influenced the age of Enlightenment as he encouraged the acceptability of studying secular subjects. The teachers of this era began to separate the discovery of natural phenomena from the pursuit of religion.

In the twentieth century, the study of classical humanities—the skills and ideas that reveal the nature of being human (as in Cicero's concept of *humanitas,* or "human nature," and the *studia humanitatis,* or "studies of humanity," of Italian humanists in the Renaissance)—was gradually replaced with man's interpretation of what was true for him alone, whether the wisdom of learned men throughout the ages supported it or not. Instead of curriculum reminding us that we can stand on the shoulders of intellectual giants, professionalized education has compartmentalized information and detached the individual from one of our greatest resources—the history of human thought. Latin, the language of science, is no longer required of science majors, as though the terms used by scientists have nothing to do with the ideas of science.

And so, the current culture of education has displaced parents as the primary instructors of children in favor of professionals who try their best to recreate the home environment at school; has the federal government rather than the community determining the structure of equal educational opportunity; has deserted the idea that memorization trains the brain; has fostered a loss of literacy by replacing the study of original writings with abridged textbooks; and has created a populace unable to engage in reasonable discourse. We have rejected the historically successful model of rigorous, classical education in favor of entertainment and job training.

Today's educators reject the importance of preparing our next generation to enter the great classical conversations of history because they no longer believe there is a core body of knowledge common to man. So personal opinion has trumped universal truth, expediency has displaced goodness, and edginess has shoved aside beauty. Families no longer know that a great classical conversation exists and that their children could become its most interesting participants.

CHAPTER TWO

WHY WE NEED CLASSICAL EDUCATION

Is it not the great defect of our education today that although we often succeed in teaching our pupils "subjects," we fail lamentably on the whole in teaching them how to think? They learn everything, except the art of learning.

—*Dorothy Sayers*, The Lost Tools of Learning

Many cultural commentators have written books that analyze the inability of today's children to master the art of learning, but few offer practical answers. The current educational confusion demands a very specific, commonsense solution that any family can implement. *The Core* advocates a proven, time-tested solution as it prescribes a plan to restore the foundations of proficient literacy and numeracy for all children. Parent-led, goal-driven, community education must replace government-led, entertainment-driven, centralized education.

Though instilling the values of a classical education might sound too lofty an aspiration, the trivium (grammar, logic, and rhetoric) is actually simple to implement if it is explained in terms analogous to the methods we naturally use to learn. Classical education encourages us that we are capable of becoming an Oxford don who builds bicycles, or a plumber who reads Milton, or a business owner who spouts theology. The classically educated are not defined by their occupation so much as by their breadth of knowledge and understanding. And the processes of a classical education are so simple that all parents and educators can competently implement a classical curriculum and challenge the intellect of any child. Remember, before universal, compulsory education, this model was taught by sixteen-year-old youths in one-room schoolhouses full of children of various ages and abilities. If these young teachers could do it, we can do it, especially today, with the multitude of tools and resources available at our fingertips.

THE WORLD IS THE CLASSROOM

When you ask someone, "What do you do?" do you really mean, "What's your job?" Can you imagine asking George Washington what he did for a living? He would have answered that he was a farmer. He worked at home, except when he wasn't at home. His role in history reveals that he could have responded, "I'm a farmer, a citizen, a stepfather, an army officer, the president, Martha's husband, etc." Even a craftsman such as a cooper or a goldsmith in colonial Boston would have farmed and constructed and participated in church and community government. For most early Americans, their daily duties were defined by the task ahead of them rather than by a particular career they had been trained for.

Global technologies offer us an opportunity to return to this way of thinking. Many Americans no longer "go to work" at a factory or office. Instead, an employee can now work all over the place—at home, on the road, at a coffee shop, in the office, and on airplanes. Adults have often wished to be able to work at home in order to spend more time with their loved ones. Recent advances in technology, the easy use of computers and access to the Internet, and the desire for effective, low-cost educational models have all inspired more adults to investigate home-centered employment, which has naturally led to their also considering home-centered education.

My family is a participant in this sociological return to home as a hub. Rob and I run our Internet business from home, our children are schooled there, and many of our business partners from around the world stay in our home. We spend part of each day completing our household chores, teaching the children, and visiting with our neighbors and their children. We determine what needs to be done each day, schedule who will be where at what time, and regroup as a family each evening. We meet clients in restaurants or through online meetings. We stop in the shipping warehouse for our online store for a few hours each day. We use the computer and phone to discuss business concerns. Our boys travel with us when we travel for work. We are in the middle of what cultural analyst William Bridges calls "jobshift" (shifting work from a factory or office back to the home through technology), and we love it.

Even though we center our children's education from home, we don't stay home. Another cultural analyst, Charles Handy, author of *The Age of Unreason,* points out, "From home is different than at home. The home is the base not the prison. We can leave it. There will be organized work clubs, work centers, meeting rooms, and conference centers. . . . It is not a lonely life" (*The Age of Unreason,* p. 178). Handy's observation applies equally to work and school.

Our sons study on their own, with us, and with tutors. They can "social nitwit" online as well as any other student, but they also choose to bring academics into their free time. On a recent excursion, held midweek while most others are in school, our boys worked on writing a screenplay with two other boys who were vacationing with us. No one asked these four boys to bring pen and paper on vacation. They just did so because they live in homes where writing is a part of life. The boys, along with a team of a dozen friends, had just finished collaborating on a play for a competition and had also participated in writing an anthology of short stories. The academic skills they learned transferred into their free time and provided them with entertainment. Learning, traveling, friends, and family are connected. Likewise, school and work and family are not three different compartments; they live an integrated life.

PARENTS AS HEADMASTERS

Some people remain skeptical that parents are capable of teaching their children. If compulsory, universal schools are effective in educating children, then I would think that it should not be difficult for each of us who attended school for twelve years to pass on the basic knowledge we learned. Is it possible we never learned the basics very well in the first place, so that we know we have nothing to offer our children academically? I know I had various forms of English courses in school for twelve years, yet it wasn't until I taught my own children to parse a sentence that I learned that we actually conjugate verbs in English. I thought that was something that I only did in French class. I never connected the study of French to real people in France or thought to look for similarities between French and the English language. I just wanted to pass the class and get a credit so I could go to college and get a job. Maybe feeling incompetent to teach the basics I studied in school is the correct response. Why would I want to send my children to a system that repeats the cycle?

Hundreds of thousands of classically minded parents, without any professional training, are successfully teaching subjects as diverse as Latin, logic, and literature to their children. They have rediscovered the simple beauty of training minds to consume copious quantities of words, facts, and ideas. The human brain is a sponge, and these parents understand that through diligent study, children are capable of mastering difficult material to the point where studying becomes a normal activity during free time.

As a leader in the home-centered education movement, I have the honor of reminding parents that they *are* competent and that they can be trusted to love their children and pass on the knowledge their family values.

Since the early 1980s, homeschooling families have consistently raised proficient readers, writers, and mathematicians. The National Home Education Research Institute provides data online that compares home-centered outcomes to institutional outcomes. Parents can do a great job—we just have to acknowledge our own deficiencies and learn alongside our children.

For the classically minded parent, quality academic material provides the content on which to practice the skills of learning. So whether a teacher, a computer, a parent, or a book requires an assignment, the parent is ultimately responsible for training the child to have the character to practice the skills necessary to complete the task. The classical educator understands that struggle is part of the learning process, expects to teach students accountability by assigning rigorous academic tasks, and uses the challenges within the assignment as an opportunity for the development of brain and character for the whole family. The goal is not to check off items on a list—one more assignment completed or one more answer given correctly. Instead, we want to teach young children how to behave so that the brain can function optimally. In other words, we know our students can provide a correct answer or reasonable solution (artifact) if they have over-practiced the tools of learning (process). A product can be referred to as an artifact. The better our art or processes, the more perfected the artifact. Creating a good or beautiful artifact is only possible when the correct process or technique is practiced. For example, if the artifact to be created is an eloquent paragraph, the student must first practice the art of constructing sentences and connecting ideas. If a student is creating a sculpture, the student must first practice the processes of sculpting. Classical educators know the artifact will only be as good as the art practiced, so over-practicing a core of learning skills is as important as finding the correct answer.

BRAIN TRAINING IS THE GOAL

Every member of my family is brain-damaged. Think about it. The continuum of brain functionality has two end points—comatose or perfect.

No one in our family is comatose. (When there were four boys in the house, however, I was grateful for sleep, when we could at least act like we were comatose.) No one in our family has a perfect brain, either. We are all functioning with brains that tend to the deficient end of the spectrum. Therefore our brains require extensive physical therapy—called education. Whether your children are absolutely brilliant or thoroughly incompetent, they all require more physical therapy.

People, whether mentally handicapped or gifted, learn through repetitive practice until a given concept is memorized. Our brain delights in acquiring information and new understanding. We learn by having our senses literally absorb data into our brain. The more we see the same information from different angles and through a variety of experiences, the more neural pathways we create to access that idea, and the easier information becomes to process or think about.

Interesting research on people with brain injuries demonstrates what scientists call the "plasticity" of the brain. The brain wants to learn. It craves learning, growth, new thinking. It cries out to be used. When the portion of the brain initially designed for certain tasks is injured, other portions of the cranium "stretch" to compensate, hence the term plasticity. If new nerve paths are worked over and over again by a physical therapist, the brain repartitions itself to take over the injured portion's function. Brains can be trained to retain, even when severely damaged. We access information from our brain most comfortably when we have developed the capacity (which involves the discipline and character) to over-learn information. If our brain is damaged in one area and we work very methodically, we can often overcome our handicaps to a greater extent than most of us realize. So even though my brain is not perfect, it can compensate for its deficiencies if I work hard.

Helen Keller is the perfect example of a person with every excuse not to learn anything due to her physical disadvantages. Deaf, blind, and mute from an illness in infancy, she still became proficient in learning how to learn. Her teacher didn't let her pupil's inadequacies or special needs limit her opportunities. When Helen was mature enough to be responsible for her own education, she knew how to wrestle with seemingly impossible tasks until she achieved her goals. She worked so hard that the healthy parts of her brain compensated for the damaged portions. Of course, the brain also gets tired, just as a baseball pitcher's arm does, and wants to stop working. Then our resolve is tested as we force ourselves to complete a task. Our attitude defines us far more than our physical abilities.

Someone else who overcame learning disabilities is Dominic O'Brien. He was the World Memory Champion for many years and has written practical, interesting books on brain functionality and techniques for learning. In the introduction to his book *Learn to Remember*, O'Brien relates a turning point in his life. After watching a memory champion in a competition, he spent three months trying to learn to duplicate the champion's efforts. Eventually, O'Brien could memorize six decks of randomly shuffled cards from a single sighting.

He writes that, after only a short time practicing, "While I was amazed and impressed by my own brain's capacity, I felt at the same time immensely bitter that I had never been taught these same levels of mental agility when I was a student struggling with examinations. As a child, I was diagnosed as dyslexic. In addition, I was described as having an inability to concentrate on and remember what my teachers were saying. As a result, I did not shine academically, and I left school at sixteen."

He goes on to ask an interesting question: "Even today, when we know comparatively so much about the brain and the processes of learning, children are not taught to learn effectively. Why? I have to confess that the answer to that question escapes me."

You may not have the ambition of Dominic O'Brien, but he asks a good question. Let's respond to the question by action and use the same processes he used. If he can become a memory master at a much older age than most of his competitors, then it is not too late for us. As we begin sharing quotes, speeches, scriptures, and poems with our children, we can help two generations at once recover the memory and recitation skills of a classically educated student.

THE CLASSICAL MODEL IS THE METHOD

Classical education is steadily gaining momentum as more and more classical schools open around the country. The Association of Classical and Christian Schools grew from 130 schools with 17,420 enrolled students in 2007 to 220 schools with 32,922 enrolled students in 2008. Likewise, many homeschool families have turned to this model. Classical Conversations had over 17,000 students and their parents enrolled in classical seminars in 2009. These are just two of many classical school associations.

So, why is classical education gaining in popularity? Because it works. Contemporary education has replaced methods that have worked for millennia with social experiments that ignore the hard work required to learn. The most prominent failed educational experiment is, of course, the abandonment of memorization and recitation, or training brains to retain and share large amounts of information. In contrast, the classical model with its focus on memorization and recitation is a proven method that has been used to train the minds of the world's finest statesmen, philosophers, scientists, and artists for over 2,500 years.

In the 1990s, I was fortunate enough to read classical educator Doug Wilson's *Recovering the Lost Tools of Learning* around the same time that John Gatto, who quit teaching in public schools after winning New York Teacher of the Year, was writing books about the ineffective teaching techniques currently used in American schools. Like many other interested parents, these authors caused me to question all that I knew about education. After looking into their historical references, I learned that good teachers had always fully understood that learning is a three-step process.

As Dorothy Sayers, a novelist and friend of C. S. Lewis and J. R. R. Tolkien, described in her essay "The Lost Tools of Learning," the novice must first behave like a parrot, repeating the basic vocabulary, ideas, and concepts of the master craftsman. Every student must learn to speak the language of the subject.

For instance, I have been trying to learn about paper quality for the various materials my curriculum company creates. I can't just order a book from a printer and expect that the product I had in mind will arrive in the mail produced at the best price. I have to learn the names of various paper weights, paper glosses, laminate thicknesses, and different margin bleeds. I need to be able to speak the way a printer thinks in order to convey the idea of the type of book I would like created from my mind to the printer's mind. Once I understand what the various printing specifications mean, I can email a file to any printer on the Internet that has the best prices and include instructions such as, "Please use linen paper at 100 lb weight, 3-hole punched, double-sided, black and white, covered with a clear 2 mm laminate," and I can be confident I'll receive the product I requested. Then I can teach the person who orders books for my company to order the specified book using the correct printer's terms. If I can teach new ideas to others using the specific language of a subject, then I am becoming educated in that field.

You have the skill to learn anything if you know how to:

1. Memorize vocabulary and rules (also called grammar)
2. Process new concepts logically (also called dialectic), and
3. Clearly explain the grammar and dialectic to others (also called rhetoric).

Classical educators teach these three basic skills, referred to by the Latin term the trivium, which, as you'll recall from Chapter One, means "the three roads" (or a place where three ways meet). Classical education is analogous to brain training. When encountering new information, the brain must know how to store data (grammar), retrieve and process data (logic), and express data (rhetoric).

GRAMMAR RESTORES MEMORIZATION SKILLS

Grammar, the first skill set to be practiced, roughly corresponds to our elementary schools, or to students up to about eleven or twelve. *Webster's Universal Unabridged Dictionary* lists grammar as general systems and principles of speech and writing (1936, p. 738, definitions 1–4). Definition five explains grammar as "An outline of the principles of any subject; as, a grammar of logic." A more contemporary dictionary, the *Oxford English Dictionary*, defines grammar as "The fundamental principles or rules of an art or science" (definition 6), citing an example from the *Times* of London (1963), "The grammar of the film was established."

A student must begin with grammar no matter their age or the topic. Grammar is essentially defined as the science of vocabulary. Every occupation, field of study, or concept has a vocabulary that the student must acquire like a foreign language before progressing to more difficult or abstract tasks within that body of knowledge. A science or system is defined, described, and organized by its vocabulary. A basketball player practicing the fundamentals could be considered a grammarian, in a sense, as he repeatedly drills the basic skills of passing, dribbling, and shooting.

Grammar schools provide practice for the memorization of the rudimentary facts of any subject. For history, an example might be the major points of a time line of Western civilization, whereas in math, this would involve the memorization of multiplication tables and geometric formulas. English memory work would include sentence structures, noun and verb endings, and parts of speech. Students memorize maps, dates, events, scientific categories, poetry, passages of prose, and much more. The students are taught to memorize by developing academic skills such as drawing charts, schematics and visual mnemonics, listening to and repeating history time lines and science facts, memorizing and reciting spelling rules and literary passages, voraciously consuming easy readers, and writing outlines and sentences. Memorization comes easily to younger students and it is critical preparation for higher-order thinking skills.

While rote memorization is currently considered unnecessary by many educators (as exemplified by the allowance of calculators before college math), classical educators consider it advantageous for two main reasons:

1. It strengthens the student's brain by straining it a little more each day, and
2. the student takes in quality content that informs an educated person.

These differ greatly from the "edutainment" offered to encourage elementary students to "enjoy" school. Classical educators prefer to prepare children to work hard at learning until the skills become enjoyable. Consider this important difference: classical teachers prefer to teach children to *like* memorizing quality content (such as a rhyme or sonnet) so that one day they can enjoy difficult assignments. We want their self-esteem to be based on actual accomplishments.

It's hard to evaluate an historian's analysis of world events if you don't know the names of the people and places and dates he's referring to. You can't appreciate the causes and events of history if you don't first know who, what, where, and when. It's hard to know if your car mechanic is dishonest or giving good advice if you can't understand his diagnosis. It can be scary to say, "The 'what' is rubbing against the 'which' when the cylinder pushes past the 'how,' and you want $600 to fix it?" Or, say you're applying for your first home loan and you keep hearing words such as "interest only," "variable rate," "amortized," and "Please sign here..." The interest-only mortgage boom in the 2000s financially destroyed many families who didn't understand basic multiplication or the meanings of the terms the sales agents were using.

How can we teach our children to memorize a broad range of information? Let me prove to you that all people are (potential) geniuses, with brains designed to store, manipulate, and retrieve large amounts of information through rote memorization. Imagine the grocery store you shop in the most. If I asked you to tell me where the eggs are so I could run right in and grab them, would you be able to do so? Of course you could. The average grocery store carries over 10,000 items, yet you can quickly tell me where to find most of them. Why? The store is organized by category, and you have shopped in the store repeatedly. In other words, you've seen those organized items over and over again, and the arrangement by category makes it easy for you to memorize the store's layout. You can categorize 10,000 items from just one store. Even more amazing, you can do the same thing in very many stores.

You also have memorized many details about every item. You know which products are fresh and which are processed. You can comprehend the ingredient labels and you can make choices based on quality and price in comparison of an item in one store to the quality and price you remember from other stores. You can go home and taste the item, determine if you like it, and then remember that sensation when you go to purchase the product again. You learn which butchers point you to the best meat and which produce managers will get you the latest shipment of fruit from the refrigerator in the store's warehouse section. You learn the store's marketing system and discover the best times to shop for the best prices. You manage whole fields of data associated with tens of thousands of items in just one of the very many stores you visit each week. You are a human data machine. You can categorize and memorize anything.

Likewise, a good grammatical education teaches a child how to build a "grocery store of the mind" for every subject. Children are not only fed information to put on the "shelves" in their minds, but they are also helped to discover ways to organize the data for quick retrieval. When the child searches for an idea or fact, she has a place where the mind's eye goes to either retrieve currently stored, related facts or to find a sensible location to "shelve" new facts for later retrieval. If your grocery store started carrying organic eggs, the manager would have to decide whether she should put them in the organic section, or with the current eggs, or maybe in a new temporary, promotional location in the front of the store until customers knew it was regularly available to buy. We need to teach our children to do the same thing with new facts. Are there multiple ways to pronounce a word? Is there more than one way to write a mathematical formula? Do I file a fact in just one place, or can I file it in multiple brain locations?

To build the brain's knowledge store, you begin by memorizing orderly systems. You do that by visiting the "store of words" for any particular subject many times in an organized manner. For a student it means repeating data (revisiting the store) in an orderly fashion (filling the shelves).

So we instruct students to repeatedly draw the same continental maps as we build the geography aisle. We repeatedly chant the same multiplication and addition tables and laws of math as we build our math aisle. Eventually, we can pull the identity law down off its shelf to use in the "balance the equation" recipe. We repeatedly list the same history time line as we build our history aisle. Eventually, we can pull down the items "Hitler," "Napoleon," and "Alexander" to mix into our analysis of despotic rulers. We work consistently over a long period of time until the difficult becomes effortless. Whenever we add a new ingredient to the memory's shelf, we already have developed a logical place for it to live.

Since rote memorization is the first step to filling the shelves, it is a good thing that children like learning lots of new words. Every child learns to speak from infancy through repetition and memorization and orderly associations. Memorized childhood favorites like the Alphabet Song, or the Pledge of Allegiance, or the Lord's Prayer stay with us for a lifetime. I am not talking about something recited for a season and then forgotten. Educated children are building a permanent, organized storage system in the brain with key ideas that they will continue to use lifelong. Some facts may turn out to be just fads, trivia that can be discarded, but children work hard to build a critical mass of information and we should provide them with the tools to support a framework of shelves that never disappears.

No matter what your children's strengths and weaknesses are, or their likes and dislikes, or their gifts and talents, their brains want to gather, sort, store, and retrieve information. The food on the shelves is useless if it is not mixed into a recipe and shared with a hungry person, but you can't feed the hungry if you can't locate the ingredients in the recipe. A goal of learning is not just to fill the shelves; it is to develop useful human beings who can use their talents in practical ways to feed the needs of fellow humans.

LOGIC RESTORES ANALYTICAL SKILLS

Training the brain to gather and store information is just the first step toward being able to think. Logic is the next stage in the trivium. We need to learn how to think abstractly in order to compare the more concrete ideas learned in the grammar stage. (The terms "logic" and "dialectic" are used interchangeably by classical educators.) Students naturally become interested in debating the merits of anything by the time they reach middle school. So, the classical model complements and exercises their natural tendencies to "talk back" by teaching young teenagers to argue effectively by using formal logic. It takes a wise parent to trust that it is appropriate to teach their young child to argue well.

As students become conversant in a subject, they learn to apply their new vocabulary in a logical context. For example, students progress from memorizing math facts and math laws to their logical application—algebra. Modern math students are shown how to cross multiply to solve for an unknown in a fraction, but classically trained students would be expected to recognize that the identity law is the rule that allows them to cross multiply. The grammar of math problem solving is specifically identified and studied so that students begin to learn that algebra is the logical application of only a few simple laws and operations already learned in arithmetic. Algebraic applications in geometry, trigonometry, and calculus are no longer treated as disconnected, abstract subjects, but as interrelated tools used to measure real objects.

A good historian goes through the same process. She learns historical grammar such as a basic time line of events that provides her with mental pegs on which to hang new information (the Renaissance followed the Middle Ages, etc.). She also memorizes maps so she can see in her mind's eye where events happened. Then she learns how to process this information. For example, why did Robert E. Lee choose to join Jefferson Davis instead of Abraham Lincoln? What events in Lee's life made him take such a stand? We can analyze Lee's decisions only if we know who he is and how he came to be that way. Geography, faith, and politics were major influences in the life of General Lee. The historian wants to logically analyze pertinent facts related to Lee in order to form coherent conclusions.

During the dialectic or logic stage, proficient readers go through the skills of decoding, comprehending, and analyzing increasingly complicated literature while simultaneously developing writing skills, particularly paragraph development. Classical educators replace excerpts, work sheets, and handouts with blank sheets of paper on which children transcribe their own knowledge, developing a culture or "habit of mind" that is able to think on paper. The grammarian learned the basic structure of words and sentences. Now it is time to teach them to put correctly written sentences into logical order with a topical paragraph. This is like the basketball player in the example above applying the fundamental skills and rules of play to team strategy.

RHETORIC RESTORES COMMUNICATION SKILLS

Rhetoric may be defined as the faculty of observing in any given case the available means of persuasion.

—*Aristotle*, Rhetoric

Grammar and logic prepare the student for rhetoric studies. Rhetoric can be defined as a course of study formalized by Aristotle and taught as a seminar in classical universities and some high schools. Rhetoric can also mean a "sound bite" or (usually political) propaganda meant to persuade a gullible public. To classical educators, rhetoric means to practice very specific skills in order to be the most persuasive in expressing truth, goodness, and beauty. Rhetoric students are able to recognize how the particulars of one specialization relate to the particulars of another. In rhetoric school, students learn to speak and write persuasively and eloquently about any topic while integrating allusions and examples from one field of study to explain a point in another. Rhetorical skills are the final tools practiced in a classical education. Once grammar, logic, and rhetoric are over-practiced, a student is prepared to study anything.

If students have really mastered the language of a field of study, we want them to be able to express the ideas they understand. But expressing yourself clearly is a difficult skill that needs to be taught and practiced, so rhetoric has its own grammar. Educators often refer to communication skills as rhetorical skills. Scholars focus on both oral and written rhetoric. Oral skills are often taught through speech and debate classes, and are sometimes called forensics. Forensics, derived from the Latin word "forum," as in court of law, actually means pertaining to legal proceedings or argumentation. Popular television shows have changed the meaning to something related exclusively to scientific investigation, as by a forensic pathologist. The term is actually much broader, as forensics implies researching an idea and then comparing it to things known by the audience in order to persuade them to one side of an argument or the other. Hence, the term "rhetoric" is closely tied to the idea of oral, documented, or physical evidence explained to the appropriate audience.

For example, a student might be reading Charles Dickens and Elizabeth Gaskell and might determine that Dickens seeks to stir up the cause of justice for the oppressed, while Gaskell is more interested in examining labor issues from the point of view of both the employer and the employed. The controversial labor issues may inspire this student to write an essay comparing the two authors' treatment of justice in the workplace. Or she might become an informed social activist with history, literature, and writing skills in her toolbox. Either way, she is inspired to meaningful, purposeful action and need not feel inept while trying to persuade others of her idea of justice. The ideas may have been imparted to her by "dead authors," but they have current applications. The student who can calmly, simply, logically, and eloquently express thoughts through words or actions is a rhetorician. By contrast, modern high schools emphasize a survey of textbooks in which the authors trivialize history and literature. A classically trained student would have the skills needed to read the original text, ask and find answers to her own questions, and clearly present her findings to her audience.

Almost any skilled person you encounter must have these tools to be successful in his or her field. For example, a good car mechanic who owns a successful repair shop is usually a great rhetorician. First, he learned the grammar of automobiles. He knows the names of all the parts of the car engine. He knows the vocabulary of his field of expertise. He is trusted because he can explain the purpose of a carburetor and a cylinder. Second, he has learned to compare, analyze, and process the facts he knows about car engines. He understands how the parts of the car work together. He can diagnose why a problem in one part of the car is making another part work improperly. The experienced mechanic learned this by spending a lot of time around cars and car magazines and car enthusiasts, and maybe even by going to auto mechanic school. He is trusted because his experience of repeatedly examining many automobiles has enabled him to easily diagnosis mechanical problems. Lastly, he learned how to express his knowledge clearly. He knows how to explain to nonmechanical people what is wrong with their car and he can even impart his mechanical knowledge to others. He is a rhetorician in the field of car mechanics when he can persuade others to keep coming back to pay him to repair their cars and when his reputation is so honestly earned that his customers recommend his services to their friends.

You can repeat the entire paragraph above by substituting the word "surgeon" for "car mechanic" and the idea of body parts for car parts. Trust comes from more than knowledge; we have trouble trusting a surgeon with a bad bedside manner. A good rhetorician knows how to share his knowledge in order to benefit the greater community.

The same thing is true in all fields: an over-practiced skill eventually becomes a delightful art to be shared. In the example of the basketball player used above, the star who effortlessly dances around his opponents while leading his whole team to victory is a kind of rhetorician. He practiced until his body hurt; he strategized and understood the rules until he could see the court and every player with his eyes closed. And now he makes the fans leap in applause as they admire his "natural" ball-handling skills. The classical educator knows that anyone could learn to think or play or create extremely well if they would just work with as much passion as a "gifted" athlete.

In every field, excellent academics require perseverance, sweat, wrestling, time, tears, and just plain labor over the *fundamentals*. If parents will practice the art of learning, even difficult subjects will become accessible to the entire family. Recovering the classical tools of learning allows each of us to tackle new disciplines, and that's when learning becomes practical and personally empowering. So, as you go about your day, see if you can break down the things you like to do into grammar, dialectic, and rhetoric skills, and then share your findings with your family.

PROFICIENT LITERACY IS THE RESULT

Proficient literacy is just the beginning of a good education. It is not the only measure, but it sure is important. Before the 1450s, when Gutenberg produced the first printed Bible, it wasn't possible for many people to be literate. Books were too rare for the masses to own until the printing press was developed, but small, highly literate segments of society did the hard work of preserving books for us by copying them by hand. Now books and online texts, both modern and ancient, are easily accessible to all industrialized nations.

Yet the only time in the recorded history of this planet that a culture has had universal, proficient literacy was in the United States from the 1600s to the 1950s. The vast majority of Americans from this era could comprehend a very broad range of vocabulary. This ability stemmed from the large amount of literary capital developed through reading the King James Bible, political periodicals and pamphlets, farming journals, and classical authors. All other cultures worldwide have produced significantly fewer proficient readers than America before the 1950s. If I am going to ensure that my children are well educated, I want to follow the model that has been proven to work for all kinds of students because each of my children is a unique individual.

Neil Postman, the author of *The End of Education*, devotes two chapters in his earlier, classic book on the effects of various media, *Amusing Ourselves to Death*, to analyzing literacy rates from the colonial era through the 1900s. He concludes, " ... there is sufficient evidence that between 1640 and 1700, the literacy rate for men in Massachusetts and Connecticut was somewhere between 89 and 95 percent. . . . The literacy rate for women is estimated to run as high as 62 percent in the years 1681–1697" (p. 31).

He proceeds to give details of the American lyceum movement throughout the 1800s, on which Alfred Bunn, a visiting Englishman, remarked, "It is a matter of wonderment ... to witness the youthful workmen, the over-tired artisan, the worn-out factory girl ... rushing ... after the toil of the day is over, into the hot atmosphere of the over-crowded lecture room" to hear intellectuals speak for hours (p. 40). Lyceums, named for the covered garden where Aristotle lectured in ancient Greece, were the popular version of today's movie theaters.

Postman also lists the quantities of the copies of various books sold in cities in comparison to the size of the population and estimates literacy rates were actually higher. In a time when books and paper were very expensive, a high percentage of Americans devoured reading material.

Laura Ingalls Wilder, in her book *Little Town on the Prairie*, wrote about a test she had to pass in the late 1800s when she was fifteen years old in order to be certified to teach in a one-room schoolhouse. Here is a small part of a long sentence she was asked to parse. In case you missed the average third-grade education given in a one-room schoolhouse, parsing just means to reduce a whole to its parts and identify them.

> "'I' is the personal pronoun, first person singular, here used as the subject of the verb 'saw,' past tense of the transitive verb 'to see.' 'Saw' takes as its object the common generic noun, 'eagle,' modified by the singular article, 'an.'"

A similar passage comes from the fictional *Rebecca of Sunnybrook Farm* in a conversation between Miss Dearborn, a country schoolteacher, and nine-year-old Rebecca. Miss Dearborn begins,

> "Now let's have our conjugations. Give me the verb 'to be,' potential mood, past perfect tense."

Rebecca responds,

> "I might have been, Thou mightst have been, He might have been, We might have been, You might have been, They might have been."
>
> "Give me an example, please."
>
> "I might have been glad. Thou mightst have been glad. He, she, or it might have been glad."
>
> "'He' or 'she' might have been glad because they are masculine and feminine, but could 'it' have been glad?" asked Miss Dearborn, who was very fond of splitting hairs.
>
> "Why not?" asked Rebecca.
>
> "Because 'it' is neuter gender."
>
> "Couldn't we say, 'The kitten might have been glad if it had known it was not going to be drowned'?"

Even though Rebecca is fictional, the author wrote the book with the expectation that nine-year-old girls would be able to appreciate Rebecca's dilemma. American nine-year-old girls have rarely even heard of conjugating verbs, let alone discussing "potential moods" outside the context of pubescent angst. The National Council of Teachers of English (NCTE) thinks it is no longer even necessary to learn how to parse a sentence because instruction in English grammar takes time away from creative writing. How does one write creatively without using proper sentence structure? Focusing on the artifact (a creative paper) rather than the process has made the leaders of this educational organization unable to appreciate the value of dissecting a sentence. Parsing allows us to correct an error in a sentence, and how to explain what part is wrong, and why. This skill also allows our citizens to discover if a politician's argument is valid and to learn foreign languages and to even write geometry proofs. A geometry proof requires us to parse and identify physical relationships among shapes, just as parsing a sentence allows us to identify the relationship between words.

In the autobiography *Mary Emma & Company*, unschooled, twelve-year-old Ralph Moody's family moves in the 1910s from the Colorado frontier of one-room schoolhouses to the graded school system of Boston. He has to take a placement test so the principal can determine which class to place him in. The principal asks, "What is the result of twelve times twelve, divided by thirteen, times five, divided by three?" Ralph responds, "I got along all right until I came to fifty-five and five-thirteenths, then I got a little bit mixed up in trying to divide it by three... I got mixed up when I got into the thirteenths..."

And so, Ralph was placed in seventh grade instead of eighth because he had spent his days providing for his widowed mother and siblings rather than sitting in school. How many adults who have attended modern schools, let alone children, can hold and manipulate that many numbers in their head? Yet it was commonly expected of all children, as evidenced by *Ray's Higher Arithmetic*, published in 1880, which was the standard math text of that time period. *Everyday Math*, a popular math curriculum in contemporary elementary schools across the United States, explains that learning multiplication tables is no longer necessary because students can simply use calculators. Modern Americans are no longer expected to mentally divide mixed numbers even by single digits, let alone by thirteenths like Ralph Moody was.

While striving for universal school attendance, education abandoned the simple skills that inculcate universal literacy. Implementing the classical model will restore all types of literacy—cultural, math, and language literacy—for all demographics just as it did when our nation was young. The educational outcomes portrayed as normal in the children's literature of an earlier era have provided me with a vision for the proficiency my own children can achieve. I have been privileged to begin recovering these skills as an adult so that I may share them with my children.

THE TRIVIUM REPLACES CAREERISM

Even though Americans are known for working hard, long hours, during times of economic trouble we can become very anxious about job security. The classical approach trains the student to become a thorough and capable learner, rather than focusing on training for a single job skill. There is nothing wrong with job training—we'll all probably need training at some time or another—but practicing the art of learning will prepare us to more easily adapt to an ever-changing world of employment options. Plumbers, politicians, and party planners all need to read, write, and do math competently, so the classical model only enhances job skills.

Parents hope to raise children who are so competent at learning that when their ability to earn a decent living is threatened, they respond to the challenge and can easily turn to another profession or even feel excitement as they restructure their income opportunities rather than feel frightened by the idea that they may lose their paycheck. An advantage of a classical education is that our competencies define us more than our job title. Parents recognize that the world has changed and that their children need to acquire basic skills that enable them to function anywhere in a variety of careers. We need to offer children a broad, freeing education that allows them to think well and to be lifelong learners. Children need to be prepared for any challenge, even for job opportunities that may not exist until well into the future.

America's senior citizens are living longer and healthier. I expect my children to be seventy years old and wondering what degree or vocation they should study for and where their next business or employment opportunity is going to take them. There is no way most of us will have enough money saved to support ourselves for thirty to forty years of retirement, especially if we are healthy and want to be active and spend money and enjoy our golden years.

So the whole idea of sending our children to community college to be trained for a single career or to track our children in high school as "math people" or to define our scatterbrained elementary students as "artsy people" limits their opportunities as it encourages them to think they are only good at one thing. Even the most gifted artist will appreciate the ability to intelligently invest her income for retirement. The artist needs to develop the communication skills needed to teach art when her hands become too arthritic to earn a living creating art. The expanding global economy forces us to think about preparing broadly for careers instead of choosing too narrow a focus too soon. Besides, students are accustomed to our fast-paced world. They are young and curious, so let's teach them the foundational tools that offer the most flexibility in approaching a variety of opportunities.

Again, we can look to the Founding Fathers for examples. Benjamin Franklin, Paul Revere, Dolly Madison, and the Adamses were each at some time farmers, politicians, educators, and business owners. We have even distorted a famous colonial praise, "Jack of all trades" to derogatorily mean "master of none." Originally, the intent was to honor a person who could meet whatever challenges arise. For an even older example of the liberally educated woman, read Proverbs 31 (especially from verse 10, "Who can find a virtuous woman?"). The woman described in the passage is a landowner, business owner, wife, and mother. She lives a fearless life that makes her family proud of her competency because she can rise to every occasion and meet every challenge.

We all have specific gifts and talents. I'm not suggesting we ignore our children's gifts in offering them a broad education. Rather, I'm advocating that a classical education provides the scope needed to apply their strengths to a wide range of tasks. So when your music-loving child moans about having to study a foreign language, remind her that Mandarin, Hindi, and Spanish are spoken by far more people on this globe than English. Be prepared to say to her, "I know you want to be a musician, but when you are eighty-two years old, you may find yourself teaching guitar in Mongolia." The classical model helps us to think globally and with foresight. Our generation can see farther around the globe than ever before. As a parent, I need to give my children an expansive vision of their opportunities.

The classical teacher is constantly aware that the *skill* of mastering grammar is paramount and the content mastered is significant only because it provides material to study. The classical model is just commonsense education and applies equally to vocational trades and scholarly endeavors. Other classical education books promote such lofty academic goals that they seem unattainable to most modern parents, even though these same goals were the norm for earlier generations of Americans. Our job as parents is to restore our own education as we translate our vision of quality academics into small, daily deeds that transform education from an endeavor that prepares humans to earn wages to the gift of a lifestyle of learning.

This book sets a high bar in the first three chapters and then brings the learning process back to earth. The grammar of a classical education is naturally divided into small attainable steps so that all forms of literacy can be restored to every student no matter what their situation in life may be. The classically trained student will rise to meet the challenge of a rigorous education.

CHAPTER THREE

HOW CLASSICAL EDUCATION CAN HELP YOU

The history and literature of dead ages emancipates us from immersion in the flood of our own hour.

—*Russell Kirk*, Eliot and His Age

CENTERING ACADEMICS FROM HOME

Parents who like to cook naturally surround their families with good food. Parents who enjoy athletics attend sporting events with their children, just as those who like fine arts often visit museums and concerts with their families. Parents who like to discover and understand new ideas model a lifetime of learning for their children. Be encouraged to think of the things you like to do and then find ways to include your children more often. Think about how you learn and why you love the things you love. Share your passions with your family.

Few of today's parents were raised in a culture of home-centered education, so expect it to occasionally be frustrating to develop. The classical model proves that it is hard to recreate something you haven't seen before. Sometimes we have to get used to being with our children. (They don't behave like adults.) Home-centered education is natural education, which means that, naturally, nothing will go quite as planned! The spontaneity of life with children can oftentimes seem fruitless, and there's never a paycheck to help soften the harder days. The rewards come in small moments of progress and success shared as a family. This is true no matter how you school your children, but the emphasis on loving to learn academics together makes home-centered education different than other forms, in that the parents are intentional in ensuring that academics are mastered.

Author M. K. DeGenova asked 122 retirees what they would do differently if they could live life over again. The responses were published in the *International Journal of Aging and Human Development*. The number one response was that they would have spent more time on their education. "Over any other area in life," DeGenova reported, "men would spend more time pursuing their education, and women would spend more time developing their mind or intellect." Repeating my education multiple times with multiple children offers the opportunity to avoid this regret for my entire family. Parents who help with schoolwork will raise children who in turn will be parents who help their own children with schoolwork.

Our older pair of sons missed the formative years of a classical education because I had never even heard of the classical model until they were about twelve years old. The benefits for our younger pair are apparent since they memorize more, read more, write more, and discuss great ideas more than my older set. The younger boys regularly parse English and Latin sentences, and think that subjects such as formal logic are studied by everyone their age. Memorizing hundreds of new words and outlining the main topics of large books are normal activities to them. The earliest difference between our two sets of children was in their playtime. My eldest two sons picked up sticks for guns and played war like other boys. My youngest two sons picked up sticks for guns and knew which general they were and what battle they were recreating.

One time a friend and I vacationed in Disney World with our very young children who were being classically educated. We were in the Hall of Presidents and very proud that our little guys, all under seven, easily recognized and named the more famous presidents in the outer waiting area. As we sat in the inner theater waiting for the show to begin, my then four-year-old son David had to sit on my lap in order to see the stage. I wept with patriotic pride as the curtain was pulled back and the array of great American leaders began their presentation. (Apparently automatons make me very emotional.) After a few moments, David whispered in my ear, "Mom, where's Harrison? I can't find President Harrison." This made me cry even harder. My little guy, who wasn't even really doing much schoolwork at the time, had been running the 43 presidents through his mind and trying to identify each face on the stage with a name. At home, he had memorized the U.S. presidents by singing a song as he pointed to their faces on a placemat. I hadn't realized how well he had paid attention. He couldn't have made the dialectic connections if he hadn't first memorized the names of the presidents.

I've had a parent tell me that her two-year-old named the cat Amenhotep due to memorizing a time line. I've had a college student tell me her algebra professor didn't believe her when she told him she didn't own a calculator and solved the math problems in her head. I've had a university president publicly praise one of my students for winning an international Moot Court competition. The model works for those who work the model.

The classical model is not just for children with above-average intellect, though. I've had many parents of children with autism and Asperger syndrome and other cerebral difficulties say, "I was told my child would never learn [fill in the blank], and this year she was a Memory Master." But the best thing that the parent of a child with a mental disability has ever said to me was, "Before we began homeschooling, my daughter had never been asked to a birthday party or sleepover. When she was in school, the kids just made fun of her. Now she has friends." Adults know that children who *choose* to work hard learn to appreciate those who *have* to work hard. A culture of rigorous learning destroys a culture of fear of the different or the unknown. A culture of families learning together allows experienced parents to teach immature children to accept and admire different types of people.

Home-centered education also encourages us to think less about a system of grades and more about the human trying to learn a new skill. Even though this book is addressed primarily to parents and teachers of elementary grades, anyone is a "first-grader" if they are learning the grammar of a new topic. For example, if a retiree decided to learn Russian, she must begin at the beginning. To study a high school–level Russian text would be difficult for a novice even though she was much older than high school students.

What exactly makes a person a high school student when learning something brand-new? A classical educator would start with an elementary book that contained limited vocabulary and focused on nouns with only a few verbs just to get a feel for the language and to assess personal academic deficiencies. Mastering some basics of the language would encourage her to keep moving instead of becoming overwhelmed.

When learning about the classical model, parents are often concerned about the lack of emphasis on understanding and application for students of elementary school age. Parents of young children have enough to teach them without feeling like a failure if their children can't research Homer and argue over Augustine's essays by age twelve. On the other hand, parents sometimes have such a desire to see measurable progress that we overestimate our children's readiness and rush them into difficult material too early. Reread the list of grammatical goals in the Introduction to *The Core*. How old are you, and have you met all of the basic goals of a grammar education? Grammar, though at a lower level in thinking ability, can still be very rigorous and challenging. For many parents, just reestablishing the authority required to teach one's own child will consume much energy. Proceed with purpose and clarity and your whole family will rapidly advance into the dialectic and rhetoric stages of learning.

Even though the academics in this book emphasize grammatical skills, I am going to assume that your children of all ages will read (or be read) good books, have good discussions, and go to interesting places. Use these natural opportunities to practice dialectic skills and foster questions, discussion, and understanding. I am also going to assume your grammar school students will recite poems and songs, write paragraphs, and explain interesting things to friends, neighbors, and relatives. In other words, grammar school students will also participate in rhetorical activities. Though the later sections of this chapter provide a vision for moving into the dialectic and rhetoric stages, don't rush into them. The most important place to begin restoring a classical education is at the grammar stage, no matter what your children's ages or abilities are. If we build a strong foundation, the rest will fall naturally into place.

ACADEMIC ACHIEVEMENTS
THROUGH GRAMMAR SCHOOL

A daring administrator could elevate the education of an entire high school in four years if he or she would implement a plan to focus on restoring grammar skills. Youths who are quick learners would probably take a year to master the grammatical frameworks of reading, writing, and arithmetic. This would enable the students to advance their research and writing skills faster than ever before. Even the average graduates would arrive at college with more knowledge about the world than most of their classmates and would have the college years to practice dialectic and rhetorical skills. Students who would normally drop out after turning sixteen (about one-third do so nationwide) would experience much higher satisfaction as they mastered meaningful content. The satisfaction of doing things well may inspire them to consider furthering their education. But even in casting this vision, I know it will be hard for parents of a tenth-grader to hand him a third-grade English grammar book. Pride gets in the way. So just tear off the cover and black out every mention of third grade before you give it to your older student. Or remind him that Winston Churchill remained in the British equivalent of fifth-grade English for four years. Of course, you'll have to explain who Winston Churchill was—among other things, a prolific author and one of the most eloquent public speakers of the twentieth century. See, everything starts with grammar—so rejoice when you get to define a term or identify a famous name.

The lists of grammar for the various subjects covered in this book are not canonical; they are just a place to begin. Some of the grammar is truly foundational with no other options, but most subjects have a variety of places to begin establishing a permanent mental framework. For instance, if you are an American, I would suggest your young children memorize U.S. presidents. If you're British, you may choose the kings and queens of England. If you're Egyptian, you may choose to memorize the pharaohs. If you're ambitious, then memorize all of them! Memorizing a list of national historical leaders provides pegs for the rest of history for your student. So, just pick a list and start memorizing.

Think about why the following excerpts from a ninth-grade classical curriculum are difficult and what they have in common that makes them difficult. Also think about what you could do to prepare an elementary student to do well in these high school topics. It helps to persevere through the seemingly insignificant, rote grammar if we can see where it will take us as schoolwork becomes more difficult.

Even though a literate person can read the words below, the sense of each passage is difficult if one is unable to comprehend what words such as "principio," "quadratic," "nook-shotten," and "didactic" mean. In order to successfully comprehend and think about ideas, I need to be able to do more than just read. Every idea from the various field of studies exemplified below requires my brain to wrestle with the vocabulary as though it were written in a foreign language. I have to grasp the words until they are

Latin: *In principio erat verbum.*

Math: A quadratic equation is a second-order polynomial equation in a single variable x: $Ax^2 + bx + c = 0$, with A not equal to 0. Because it is a second-order polynomial equation, the fundamental theorem of algebra guarantees that it has two solutions. These solutions may be either real or complex.

History: "The British Constitution was to Montesquieu what Homer has been to the didactic writers on epic poetry" (*Federalist No. 47*, James Madison, January 30, 1788).

Literature: Shakespeare, *Henry V*, Act 3, Scene 5

> DAUPHIN: O Dieu vivant! shall a few sprays of us,
> The emptying of our fathers' luxury,
> Our scions, put in wild and savage stock,
> Spirit up so suddenly into the clouds,
> And overlook their grafters?
> BOURBON: Normans, but bastard Normans, Norman bastards!
> Mort de ma vie! if they march along
> Unfought withal, but I will sell my dukedom,
> To buy a slobbery and a dirty farm
> In that nook-shotten isle of Albion.

familiar and natural to use. This is why classical educators emphasize language arts, including maths and sciences.

I believe one of the reasons why American students don't do as well academically as those in other countries is because our schools and families don't expect us to learn multiple languages from an early age. We expect everyone else to speak English like us! So the students in other countries are privileged to consistently wrestle with foreign words from an early age. A popular joke mocks our limitations:

What do you call someone who speaks three languages? Trilingual.

What do you call someone who speaks two languages? Bilingual.

What do you call someone who speaks one language? American!

There are lots of difficult issues to resolve with globalization, but the ability to learn the language of an immigrating workforce should not challenge a truly educated populace. We should know how to learn to conjugate verbs in any language, just as colonial students were expected to master Greek and Hebrew and Latin in high school. We should expect today's students to be familiar with at least Spanish if not also Mandarin and Farsi.

In Colonial Heights, Virginia, south of Richmond, the public schools enroll students who speak Spanish, Korean, Vietnamese, and Mandarin.

"Knowing one language doesn't even prepare (the teacher)," said Kerry Robinson, director of Instructional Administration. The U.S. has a shortage of teachers, so the US Departments of Defense and Education have teamed up to train retiring military personnel to be tomorrow's school teachers through the Troops to Teachers (TTT) program. American teachers speaking Mandarin? Retired soldiers receiving bonuses to teach? Parents must really think in new ways in order to prepare their children for a world very different from the 20th century. (*The* [Colonial Heights] *Patriot,* Feb. 16, 2007)

Shakespeare, the dramatist, recognized the power in habitually memorizing and delivering words rich with potent meanings. Aeschylus wrote that words are the balm that creates a healthy mind. I would add that the study of words prepares us for a global economy by increasing our powers of thought and observation while providing even the most average of students with the ability to learn to think well, even in multiple languages.

ACADEMIC ACHIEVEMENTS
THROUGH LOGIC SCHOOL

Instead of assuming that middle school is just a playground of hormones run amok, the classical mind recognizes the strength of these physical urges and the students' need to discover individual confidence within peer appreciation. The classical model takes advantage of the students' natural desire to be with friends and assigns lots of group and team projects. We also capitalize on their desire to argue and talk back and insist they practice doing so *logically and considerately.* Instead of focusing only on grammar or pushing them into extensive research, as they will be equipped to do in rhetoric school, we concentrate on improving dialectic skills through Socratic circles, formal logic, policy debate, mock trial, collaborative stories, and time line synthesis. Adolescent scholars actually enjoy the challenge of conquering difficult subjects if they can do so with like-minded friends.

Dialectic skills are formally taught through debate, algebra, and science experiments, but the skills are also practiced with puzzles, discussions, and group interaction led by an enthusiastic thinker, because the dialectic or logical processes are really just thinking skills. I stay away from the overused term "critical thinking skills" in favor of teaching "clear reasoning skills." Classical teachers are far less interested in hearing a student's opinion or criticism than in having him or her explain the *foundation* for the opinion. We want children to recognize the difference between expressing an opinion and developing a logical conclusion through induction or deduction. That doesn't mean they can't or don't express feelings or opinions. They just need to recognize that it is a feeling or opinion. I know as an adult that it is easy for my criticisms to be formed by emotions rather than facts and/or well-reasoned ideas. So when I am tutoring older students, I encourage them to think and express their ideas clearly so we can really appreciate their point of view.

The easiest way to teach dialectic or logical thinking is to re-present the students with rules and examples they already know, help them see the relationship between the new and old ideas, and then give the scholars the opportunity to form their own conclusions about additional rules or logical outcomes. For instance, when I'm tutoring Latin, I use the grammar rules the students have already learned in English to help them discover

the rules of Latin. At the same time, they are memorizing Latin grammatical rules to facilitate that "Aha!" moment when they see how the rules
from both languages intertwine. The student who has memorized many
rules when young has a head start on the student who has to both memorize the rules and think about the logical connections for the first time.

For example, I may write the words "who" and "whom" on the board,
and tell the students that "who" is the subject noun (also called the nomi-
native) and that "whom" is the direct object noun (also called the accusa-
tive). If we add an "m," we change the word from the subject noun to the
direct object noun. Therefore, "who" becomes "whom." Next I'd write the
Latin words "puella" and "puellam" on the board and ask the students to
tell me which Latin word for "girl" is the direct object and which is the
subject noun. I may lead them to the correct observation the first few
times by saying, "If we add an 'm' to 'who' in order to make 'whom' the direct object, what do you think might be a clue for the Latin direct object?"
Since we added an "m," puellam is the direct object. So we can establish a
preliminary rule that adding an "m" indicates the word is a direct object.

More Latin examples may confirm or disprove our preliminary rule.
Eventually, we don't have to think so hard about direct objects because we
recognize that every time we see a noun end with an "m" in Latin, it is
probably a direct object, until we learn more Latin and more declensions.
Then we discover more rules for words that end in "m" in Latin. We have
to hold all those rules in our head as we translate Latin passages into English. Again, our mental dexterity is stretched and challenged. It's a good
thing we were making our students memorize so many things in grammar
school! In the dialectic stage, students are expected to sort and synthesize
the memorized rules, and properly apply their knowledge in order to increase their understanding of a subject. They are *thinking*. The dialectic
skills are easier to teach if the student has a firm core of grammar to associ-
ate with new ideas. Families practice something as difficult as Latin, not
just because Latin is useful, but because it is hard and makes them think
hard! As students become more experienced in looking for similarities and

can form their own analogies, they will need their parents' help less and less, and will even be able to formulate their own rules of language.

It is important to remember that language is language no matter what the subject matter, so below is an example of the dialectic process from the math portion of the old SAT (Scholastic Aptitude Test, or Scholastic Assessment Test, a college board exam). The classical skills are equally applicable to math, though many classicists miss this important point in the confusion between studying classical literature and learning the classical model.

Please take the time to think through the problem and notice how you use memorized math facts to teach yourself a new concept. Saying the equations out loud is a trick to quicker understanding, as speaking while you read requires the use of the mouth, eyes, and ears. Try it.

I want to teach you a new function called "at," represented by the @ symbol.

Example 1
$3 \times 3 = 9, 2 \times 2 = 4$, and $9 + 4 = 13$
is defined as the same as $3 @ 2 = 13$

Can you see a pattern?
Here is another example of the same function.

Example 2
$4 \times 4 = 16, 5 \times 5 = 25$, and $16 + 25 = 41$
is defined as the same as $4 @ 5 = 41$

Can you see that the answers to the first two equations are added in the third equation?

Now, can you tell me the answer to $3 @ 5$?

In other words, can you take the two examples of a rule and apply it to a new problem? Can you compare what you already know with a new definition and gain new understanding? How strong are your powers of observation? Can you see the patterns? Were you taught to look for patterns of thought in school?

You should understand that

$$3 \times 3 = 9 \text{ and } 5 \times 5 = 25 \text{ and } 9 + 25 = 34; \text{ therefore } 3 @ 5 = 34.$$

In order to define the new rule of "@," we had to

1. use our addition, multiplication, and equality definitions from our brain's math shelf;
2. sequentially and logically think through each step of the examples;
3. while holding previously learned definitions in our head; and
4. then apply what we observed to a new symbol.

In the process, we developed an understanding for the definition of "@." Can you make up your own problem for "@" and teach it to someone else? If you can, then you have demonstrated that you actually understand the idea of "@." In practicing "@," you will be practicing the same skills needed to become proficient at solving functions such as sine and cosine. Like "@," sine and cosine are only words; maybe unfamiliar, abstract terms, but just terms like "cat" and "mud."

The dialectic most easily occurs while "dialoging" with a student. A live person is preferable to a machine or book. Think of the math example above. I am trying to persuade you to understand a new definition. If you still don't know how to use my made-up @ operation, don't you wish you could call me and ask me to explain it to you? You know you are smart enough to understand the operation; if you could just have someone help you "see" how the symbol works, learning would be much easier. If you are struggling with the @ symbol, grab a child and work it out together before you read the rest of the book. Just by explaining the examples to someone else you will understand the operation better. One reason why large classes and computers are ineffective at this stage is that the dialectic is the hardest part of thinking, and it helps to have a face to share ideas with.

Thinking—critically or clearly—is the action the brain does when comparing more than one piece of grammar. Once, on a visit to a science center, I pointed out an eerie-looking hologram to my seven-year-old son William. He was thoroughly uninterested and he ran by to find a friend, but as he acknowledged my finger pointing at the display, he said, "Yeah, refraction, reflection, and spectrum," which he knew were the properties of light. As a mother, I just thought the hologram was cool. My son was just popping off memory work that the hologram reminded him of. William saw his first real hologram, remembered the properties of light, noticed that the hologram was a distortion of light, and made the connection. Three previously unrelated ideas in his brain are now synthesized into a single idea at almost the speed of light. Amazing how fast we are able to think!

This example also demonstrates that the dialectic, and even the rhetorical processes of learning, are not tied to any specific age or grade, but happen to all of us all the time. When William looked at the hologram, he immediately applied a core fact about light without anyone telling him to. Because he was a little boy, I had no expectation that he really understood refraction, reflection, and spectrum. I just trusted that the properties of light are a good thing for a scientist to memorize. He surprised me just as David did in Disney's Hall of Presidents. William recognized the properties and used the proper vocabulary because he had memorized facts from major scientific categories. As a first-grader memorizing that fact, it didn't seem very useful at the time. Now that he is in high school studying concepts in physical science, the memorized properties of light are very useful.

In the dialectic stage, the grammar is put to work and the challenging questions start to emerge. Now that we have looked at examples of the leap from grammar to dialectic in math, language, and science, let's look at an example from history. The grammar of history is going to be pretty similar to anyone actually trying to find out the facts, but the dialectic is where most of our disagreements become apparent. For instance, we all agree that Columbus sailed to the Americas in 1492 while commanding the *Niña,* the *Pinta,* and the *Santa Maria.* But describing and understanding his purposes for going, his actions upon landing, and the results of his expedition depend on our ability to understand his point of view and to know how our own perspective affects our understanding of his motives.

We can't begin to assess or understand Columbus's actions if we don't first agree on the facts—the basic grammar. So the dialectic student learns to stop and say, "Define your terms" before an unnecessary argument ensues. Once we agree on the meanings of terms, such as "colonization" or "exploitation," we can argue more clearly and think about our opposition's point of view before determining whether Columbus was motivated as a heroic explorer or a gold digger or something else.

The questions who, what, when, and where usually provide grammatical answers. We are able to answer the most important of dialectic questions—"Why?"—after the other questions are answered. "Why?" often requires uncomfortable assessment, understanding others' viewpoints, and determining our own ideologies and how they influence our thought processes. "Why?" is a very big question. Fortunately we can start teaching children with smaller versions of "Why?" such as, "Why do we keep the same denominator in addition?" Or "Why does refraction make it difficult to spear a fish in a river?"

Successfully asking and wrestling through the answers to these questions requires one person to help another appropriately question information, consolidate many ideas, and develop logical conclusions. Parents already help their children with these basic skills when determining lessons around allowances, time spent with friends, and the negotiation of chores. We just need to apply these same skills to school subjects because eventually the student will learn to aptly use grammar and dialectic skills as they move into the rhetoric stage.

ACADEMIC ACHIEVEMENTS
THROUGH RHETORIC SCHOOL

We have a long tradition of verbal debates in the United States, the most famous series of which are the Lincoln-Douglas debates of 1858 that catapulted the lanky lawyer from Illinois into the nation's spotlight. There is an art to verbal communication that in today's culture we relegate to the province of law and political professionals, forgetting that we are all citizens responsible for self-governance. Academic achievement in rhetorical skills is part of the bigger liberal arts package that helps many young people, whether they go into teaching, finance, journalism, business, or medicine.

In rhetoric school, which approximates high school and college, classically trained students are expected to use their developed memorization abilities to quickly master and expound upon new fields of knowledge. Defining terms and mastering vocabulary allows them to research, analyze, and synthesize new material with greater ease. During the rhetoric stage it is reasonable to assign a student a paper or speech on the ethics of stem-cell research or the witticisms of Jane Austen in comparison to Hilaire Belloc. Emotion surrounding politically charged topics can be separated from facts of nature or the history of law instead of confusing opinion with intellectual analysis. Grasping the vocabulary of wit, understanding the pun or an allusion, and introducing fellow classmates to new figures of speech requires an intellect that the rhetorical student seeks to sharpen through academic duels. Once their maturing minds are practiced at logically asking and answering big questions, students learn the canons of rhetoric—invention, arrangement, style, memorization, and delivery.

Even rhetoric has its own lingo. *Invention* concerns finding something to say, while *arrangement* is the order in which the things are said. *Style* concerns how things are said; *memorization* is about knowing what one will say; and *delivery* concerns how it will be presented. The canons of rhetoric will not be expounded upon in this book, but they are considered basic skills to be mastered by a classically trained mind. You can see how important the grammar stage is to developing the skills of rhetoric. When preparing to persuade or teach someone, we need to use words that will provide clarity. We need to know how to use the most precise words to reach our particular audience with our message. We must outline key words in an appropriate order, and we should know whether to choose folksy or scholastic types of words. We need to store many of these ideas in our memories not in order to deliver a word-for-word speech, but so that we can easily add to our speeches as our audience reacts. And we need the appropriate words to fit with our delivery. A poem or song very often requires changes in sentence structure, while an academic essay will get a higher grade if all the parts of speech are in their proper places.

As families recover rhetorical skills, students will come to value all the previous effort it took to study the grammar of basic subjects. The grammar described later in this book was chosen because it is foundational to the subjects a rhetorical student typically studies. Even if students don't study the canons of rhetoric in high school, they will still have to read and write papers, work in labs, and organize their thoughts. High school students can't be expected to readily recall the data they learned in grammar school if they don't continue to keep it fresh in their brains by using it in their discussions and written assignments. It is essential to continue the review of memory work through high school if we want geography, history, science, and other subject areas to be integrated into their high school assignments.

As rhetorical students, young scholars will have the framework of language mastered. I expect them to use it to expand their reading and writing skills to include all the major Romance languages: Latin, Spanish, Portuguese, French, and Italian. I tell my students that they can't appreciate the best jokes in Shakespeare if they can't keep up with his Latin and French, all of which were understood by the common people who attended his performances. Surely our students can be at least as fluent in multiple languages as the raucous crowds of Elizabethan London.

Students also continue to practice the dialectic skills while learning to be good rhetoricians. A true rhetorician won't just blurt out an opinion. They will weigh their words, saying the right words in the right way at the right time in order to most effectively move the listener. And here is where we must be most careful. Hitler was a great rhetorician, though of course he used his skills of persuasion in a wholly irresponsible way. For my family, it is not enough to practice the trivium; the trivium must be plumbed, or measured by truth, goodness, and beauty. These qualities are part of Aristotle's natural categories. My purpose in home-centered education is to raise children who exhibit self-control, compassion, and statesmanship when displaying or exercising knowledge. I believe the ultimate goal in a classical education is to lead a child through knowledge and understanding to wisdom and virtue. If they use their knowledge exclusively for their own purposes, I have failed.

A RENAISSANCE OF
LIBERALLY EDUCATED CITIZENS

Renaissance means rebirth, and the era known as the Renaissance was considered a time of recovering knowledge that had been previously lost to the masses (and even to the educated elite). This is exactly what I am advocating again: a recovery. Besides the rediscovery of the ancient classical texts and their reapplication to modern concerns by the average citizen, I am also advocating that classical education is most easily recovered in the same context as the heroes of the previous Renaissance—at home.

The classical model works for moderns. Graduates of classical home schools have been accepted to a diverse array of colleges and universities such as Wake Forest, Duke, Hillsdale, Grove City, Patrick Henry, Chapel Hill, West Point, Lee, Wofford, Clemson, and Georgia Tech, and usually with scholarships. It's rewarding to see the successes of these students on a practical level and to know that they can compete with the best of students from all forms of education. But the unseen participants are the parents who didn't receive scholarships but worked through the same texts with their children.

To pursue a renaissance in classical learning requires one to appreciate its usefulness for adult life. One thing that has turned some families away from the classical approach is its emphasis on language, logic, and literature instead of job skills. It doesn't seem very practical to study a "dead" language, and formal logic sounds like a difficult college course. Let me assure you that Latin is not dead; ask any doctor, pharmacist, lawyer, or literature scholar. And although I agree it is difficult to study formal logic, it is certainly practical to do so. But classical educators teach subjects not because they are practical, but because they also train people to think clearly about difficult issues.

Even if you are a very quiet person who would rather listen than speak, there are times when you must communicate to earn a living or purchase a product or enjoy a relationship. Using good descriptive vocabulary also reduces conflict. Husbands and wives would fight less often if they chose their words more wisely. Children would understand their parents' expectations better if instructions were clearly provided on how to make the bed or do the dishes. The classical model consists of teaching the grammar of manners and common courtesy.

An accomplished chef actually is an accomplished rhetorician, as is a ballerina or a composer. They have mastered the vocabulary of their field—words such as "soufflé," "plié," or "forte." Artisans have practiced their craft until they understand how all the details combine into a perfect component. The same is true for a word-crafter. She needs to know the meanings of words and their relationship to one another before she can put them into a story. When we are passionate about an art, we like to share our enthusiasm with an interested public.

I believe that the average student today can be at least well versed in a wide variety of subjects as Da Vinci or Bacon or Franklin if we stop specializing in subjects too early and expect students to apply the tools of learning to all areas of knowledge. Acquiring that knowledge is much easier now that we have a wealth of information available to all through the Internet.

APPROPRIATE USE OF GLOBAL TECHNOLOGIES

Technocrats and entrepreneurs daily use computers to start companies and to take courses in conjunction with citizens from all over the globe. Many adults make home the center of their postsecondary education by taking advantage of online universities and distance learning courses. Adults have infinite options for the advancement of learning at their fingertips. If technology is changing the way adults interact with one another, you can be sure our children's lives will be affected too. Since wireless technology has given adults the world as a classroom, why shouldn't our children have the same advantages? There are already public schools that will give students a laptop if they will stay home and study the state's coursework remotely. With the growing budget crisis in public education, it's cheaper for schools to not have to construct and maintain buildings for students. Machines are less expensive than real teachers. The low cost and high access of global technologies will change the structures of education. The Hoover Institution, a think tank at Stanford University, issued a study in March 2008 predicting that by 2019 half of all courses in grades 9 to 12 will be delivered online.

The opportunities of global technologies are also driving many families to consider home-centered education for their children. One day, it will be possible to have a hologram of a great math professor from another continent stand in your living room and instruct your family. My older boys already take online college courses within their university setting, and I studied for my doctorate through a distance learning program. Modern work and management gurus such as Peter Drucker and William Bridges, along with famous technocrats like Bill Gates and Michael Dell, promote the use of computers to develop individualized instruction that can move a student from one level of mastery to the next. The world's experts and resources are ours. These factors will encourage more parents to expect their children to take advantage of the same opportunities.

As valuable as technology is to education, we still need to heed Marshall McLuhan's warning that "the medium is the message." The media will shape the message to its own natural center. Our children are complex organisms, however, not machines, and they have an inherently different center. Computers can only ever be a *part* of one's education. With all of our inexpensive technologies, we should be able to recover the high, historic literacy our country once enjoyed when classrooms had only chalk and a slate, as Laura Ingalls Wilder did when she was a teacher on the frontier. But I would caution that children would be better educated if they weren't allowed to use computers for academics until they were proficient readers and writers with just pen and paper. The proliferation of technology has coincided with overall lower levels of literacy. Mark Bauerlein in *The Dumbest Generation* provides over two hundred pages of statistics and explanations demonstrating that for all the educational opportunities that computers provide, most users only read headlines or look at pictures on the way to social "nitwitting," as my sons call social networking. The new ease with which we can access information is wonderful, but it is becoming increasingly clear to parents that educating children requires a *relationship* between humans. We need to carefully consider the ways children use computers.

Technology can bring the best of information to your home and even provide access to great teachers through audio and video, but it is one-sided. I can yell at the annoying "talking head" all I want on the cable news show, but he can't hear me. Learning is a two-way street. You can't fully rely on technology to help your child learn, unless you actively participate with the technology, too. Suppose your child is studying geometry and the computer program explained everything well through the first nine Euclidean propositions. But now, the student is struggling with the tenth proposition.

If the parent or facilitator is unfamiliar with the first nine proofs, it will be hard to help the student when he or she comes to you with questions on the tenth proof. Parents often conclude that a curriculum is lacking or that their child is not good at a subject when in fact learning requires a mentor, an adult who can answer unprogrammed questions.

As much as I love technology and think it has value in education, most real learning comes from wrestling with big ideas and arguing with another person. New technologies force us to anticipate all the exciting changes we can imagine in a different world, but they also can rob us of the relationship between a student and his mentors. Tweets and text messaging alone just won't do. I don't have to know how to solve every problem or read every piece of assigned literature with my children, but I do need to know how to help them sort through information as they find an answer. Just talking aloud to an interested adult who's not afraid or too busy to help can often be enough for an engaged student to solve a problem.

Educators often say that the basics are being crowded out by the large number of other subjects taught in schools, such as computer technology. They argue that there is more to teach in the twenty-first century than ever before. The world is closer, scientific discovery has escalated, and technology has captivated our youth. These realities provide an even stronger argument for teaching reading, writing, and arithmetic above anything else. Tackling the basics allows students to confidently meet any new challenge. I want my family to be aware that each thing we do replaces something else we could be doing, and we must fight hard not to choose the path of least resistance. Modern technologies will not be allowed to dictate how we think. Instead, we will use new technologies appropriately rather than incessantly. The machines work for us, not the other way around. I'd prefer my children to recognize that the computer is for games and their brain is for thinking. Their brains are much more powerful.

I am not against using technology for school; I am just against bad educational models that don't look at a child as a whole being. We need technology to access experts and information from around the world. But most of all we need a model that inspires students to study diligently with committed tutors and parents, instead of shuffling children from room to room, book to book, and subject to subject—or computer to computer. We need to model discipleship, especially for our most endangered children. We need to consider the child as a whole human being.

LIFE ACHIEVEMENTS
THROUGH WISDOM TRAINING

One day a parent who was struggling with her college-age children asked me, "How do you raise children who *want* to work at a career, earn college degrees, follow investments, and serve their community, let alone *can?*" She's not alone in her concerns. *Newsweek* reported in 2008 that by age 30 only about 30 percent of men were bearing adult responsibilities, compared to 70 percent of the men in 1960. This concern affects not just a family like mine with four sons, but also families with young women who want to marry and build a stable family.

A college-age student—male or female—who is classically educated knows the history of mankind, has spent time studying the consequences of irresponsibility without having to behave irresponsibly, has experienced the advantages of mathematical competency, and has the ability to evaluate their talents, their skill sets, and direct their strengths into any career. Most students who have really studied subjects such as logic, advanced math, and foreign languages prove to be diligent in other areas as well. As students develop natural competencies, they desire more mature challenges.

But competency is not enough. If we leave our students with just knowledge and power, we will have fed the mind, but we will leave them with thin souls. My friend Andrew Kern, founder of the CiRCE Institute, which apprentices classical headmasters, says, "Education is the cultivation of wisdom and virtue, and it is accomplished by nourishing the soul on truth, goodness, and beauty." Kern makes the point that knowledge leads to power and, as Lord Acton stated, "Absolute power corrupts absolutely."

Many knowledgeable, powerful leaders have destroyed whole cultures with their ability to intellectually manipulate the masses and impress citizens with charismatic arguments. Knowledge and power are inadequate. That's why Kern points us forward to wisdom and virtue, the classical purpose of education. The classics are known to elevate our souls, to inspire us to arise beyond the everyday, and to intelligently question the great thoughts and actions of mankind. The goal of a classical education is not to raise "pointy-headed" scholars, but to raise a culture of clear thinkers.

Kern reminds us of another reason why parents are the best equipped to lead their children. Ultimately, "the desire of every boy is to be a man and the desire of every girl is to be a woman." Time will grow their bodies even if children are utterly abandoned by adults, but too many adults behave as large children rather than mature men and women. The best way to train up a child to maturation is to have boys spend time with men and to have girls develop strong relationships with women, just as an apprentice spends time with a master. Families are designed to implement this important task by spending time with one another. I want my boys to have productive careers or be successful leaders, but I want the men they spend time with to teach them more than the tools of learning. I also want the men they know to teach them to be good, true, and beautiful. The only way there is a chance this will happen is for my husband and the men they spend time with to also be pursuing the true, the good, and the beautiful.

Introducing good music, beautiful artwork, and true words that beseech my children to look beyond popular culture is hard work. Pop culture is popular because it is easily accessible. My family enjoys pop culture—we sing rap in the car and laugh at *King of the Hill* reruns. We will always have pop culture, so let's appreciate it, but let's be wise enough to recognize its limits. Reach for the classical music station or National Public Radio when driving around town. Turn off the TV and read Jack London's adventure stories. Take art and ballroom dance lessons as a family and be sure to ask another family to join you. Any parent, regardless of educational background, can set the example of reading, listening, and viewing classical art and literature. Once parents cultivate an interest, it is not so hard to snuggle up to a youngster and share a moving quote, or close one's eyes and listen to some invigorating Vivaldi.

We can only appreciate the academic skills that allow us to appreciate truth, goodness, and beauty by doing the work required to cultivate these qualities in our own lives. Teaching subjects like algebra or history classically is actually an easy task compared to cultivating rich lives. Inspiring children to become competent, confident, trustworthy statesmen, business leaders, and parents requires a lot of help. That's why classical educators are so glad to have centuries of great narratives and investigations to draw from. Developing a culture that values the classical arts is just the first step in restoring a modern-day renaissance.

PART TWO

THE CORE OF
A CLASSICAL
EDUCATION

CHAPTER FOUR

READING

Once you learn to read, you will be forever free.

—*Frederick Douglass*

PROFICIENT READING SKILLS

The best way to develop proficiency in anything is by devoting energy to the topic. Just like people who take immersion language courses or join community orchestras in order to improve their skills, those who want to have a rich, expansive vocabulary spend time with books that have a large and varied word-stock. If we want our children to love reading, they need to spend time with people who also love reading. According to the National Endowment for the Arts' 2007 report *To Read or Not To Read,* the common factor shared by all proficient readers is that they live in households that contain over a hundred books.

Just a few books don't make a difference. If someone sacrificed time and money to acquire a large collection, books must be important to that member of the household. It follows that someone with that kind of love of books couldn't help but want to share their passion with others. It doesn't matter if their parents are rich or poor, blue-collar or white-collar, single or married; as long as there are a large number of books in the house, children will eventually become proficient readers. Parents have a responsibility to improve their own reading skills and broaden their own appetites for reading by bringing books into the home. The best way to improve your child's reading ability is by improving your own.

Fortunately, you can deepen your own understanding of literature while helping your children learn to read. Children need to spend time with books in three ways:

1. **Being read to from books above their reading level to increase speaking vocabulary.** A good reader of any age benefits by being read to, as it will also broaden their listening skills. We have an easier time reading hard words that we are used to hearing and saying.

2. **Reading easy books below level in order to master common words.** Reading below level increases speed and accuracy and should be the type of reading any of us spend the most time on. It is slow work to read a book that requires you to use a dictionary on every page. Children are naturally drawn to chapter books as they become advanced readers. I think it is important to let them read the entire *Star Wars* or *Nancy Drew* series if your children enjoy them because it makes them over-practice easy words. Being able to read easy words without expending energy frees their brain to tackle more difficult vocabulary.

3. **Reading books at a comfortable level to gently increase the child's reading skills.** Students need to read in short stints at grade level in order to stretch their reading ability. This type of reading requires a dictionary or an older reader listening nearby to help with new words. This type of reading should be read out loud or discussed to evaluate

the students' comprehension. Reading at this level also compensates for all the easy literature as it forces the student to incrementally mature his or her reading selection.

Even proficient readers need to practice reading at all three levels.

Reading as a family is the most effective way to practice all these levels of reading, whether you have one child or a large family. Our family regularly reads together two times a day, and as individuals throughout the day. As each family member reads out loud, they are practicing enunciation, pronunciation, and public speaking, as well as expanding vocabulary and reading speed. Reading aloud allows you to share funny lines or important phrases with people engaged in the same story while the ideas are fresh in your head.

The ability to read well and to love words requires some foundational skills. The easiest way to teach anyone of any age to read well is to know how to decode phonics, explain spelling rules, and define words. These are often called word attack skills. As word attack skills increase, so does reading comprehension. This builds the student's confidence to tackle even harder words in more difficult materials.

Teaching core reading skills is best done *alongside* rather than in front of a student. This is a great time to bond with your children. Especially when they're young, pull them onto your lap or put an arm around them as you encourage them to read difficult books out loud. Touch helps to break down fear and self-doubt and any other emotional barriers. Often our struggles stem from a lack of emotional confidence. It will help you encourage your child as it's hard to get frustrated with someone you are cuddling with. It's a good thing children can learn to read while they are still small.

TEACHING THE STRUCTURE OF PHONICS

Classical educators prefer to teach children to think in structures so they have a foundation to build upon. Rather than have a student memorize tens of thousands of "sight words," we teach our students to memorize about 70 sounds associated with letters and approximately 30 spelling rules that tell him or her how to combine the sounds into syllables and build words. As the sounds and spelling rules are mastered, the ability to read increasingly longer words becomes much easier. If you aren't familiar with the basic phonograms and spelling rules of English, you will want to work through a good phonics program yourself. Phonics as a method associates a single sound with a symbol called a phonogram. For instance, "b" represents the first sound in the word "boom," so the symbol "b" is a phonogram. Phonogram literally means "written sound."

American pioneers taught phonics, handwriting, and spelling rules using any book they had in the house. The text used is inconsequential if the teacher already knows the basics of reading. One reason why reading is considered a basic skill is that anyone who can read should be able to teach reading to another. The text used doesn't matter. If you understand phonics, you could scratch a word in the dirt with a stick and teach a child to read the word.

An educated person is not someone who knows something, but someone who can explain what they know to others. Americans used to expect that the core knowledge they learned from their parents was to be passed on to the next generation. I'm happy when my students get the correct answer to a question, but I am even happier when they can explain the answer. I want to know that the time my students spend learning is useful for themselves and the next generation. So over-teach the basics of reading because high levels of literacy make it easier to develop competencies in many other areas of life. The ability to break a word down into its foundational components expands one's reading skills and allows us to teach reading to another person.

I recommend studying *The Writing Road to Reading* because the author's methods gave me the ability to teach the fundamental components of reading and spelling, and the book has been popular for the last twenty-five years in the homeschooling movement. The author's techniques work and are the foundation for the kind of instruction given to students who may have cognitive difficulties. When teaching children with learning disabilities, the fundamentals need to be practiced repeatedly in order to overcome their handicap. Students who find reading to be easy should learn the same fundamentals. Understanding the core of phonics and spelling will launch students to ever-increasing heights.

As a classical educator and a busy parent, I want to grab every teachable moment. Thanks to our studies in phonics and spelling, any words my children are struggling with can be used as a quick review of phonograms. Sometimes we make funny connections, like for the phonogram 'eigh.' We call it the Greek 'a' sound. I don't know that it has a thing to do with the Greek language, but when one of my young boys calls out, "How do you spell neighbor?," I can respond, "Use the Greek a!" and they can spell the word correctly.

In order to read, the brain initially connects sounds to a symbol in a sequential order. Let's look at some basic phonics and reading skills. The following example may look like gibberish, just as written symbols look like nonsense to a nonreading child, so bear with me for their sake.

Try to read the following sentence:

?!? 40) ?@?

You can't read it unless I tell you the sound that goes along with each symbol. Now compare those words in gibberish to the same phrase in English:

Tit for tat.

In this language, '?' stands for 't'; the '!' stands for 'i'; the '@' stands for 'a'; and so forth.

You can read, and therefore potentially spell, "Tit for tat" in these strange symbols once someone tells you the sound that is associated with each squiggle or letter. In fact, I'll bet you can spell "fat" and "fort" in the strange symbol language now that you know the code. Try it.

Some students seem to teach themselves to read well without much effort. That is probably because somewhere in their early instruction someone showed these natural readers that each symbol represented a sound and from then on the child was able to crack the code without much help. Some educators think these children are sight readers, but that is usually not the case. Our brains are wired to make sense out of patterns. When we read, we are looking at a series of phonograms (letters) that connect to sounds that form a word that connects to an idea in our head. The phonograms form regular patterns within syllables, so once a natural reader understands that there is a phonetic code, they can often draw meaning from words without much help. After all, there are only 26 letters that combine to make about 70 phonograms, and most syllables only use three or fewer phonograms. The student may not even be aware that she is cracking a code because she has been associating commonly written words with sounds like "mall" or "McDonald's" since infancy. She may already be aware of the visual symbols connected to sounds and language patterns in her culture. Just as there are musical prodigies, there also exist various levels of reading prodigies.

For clarity, let's parse the word "phonogram" using phonics and spelling rules. It has 3 syllables: phon, o, gram. The first syllable, phon, consists of 3 phonograms: Ph, o, n. Ph represents the sound "f" like in "fish," o is short like most single vowels *not* at the end of a syllable, and n represents the sound made when you push your tongue to the roof of your mouth and vibrate through your nose. (Try it.) The second syllable, o, is long because the vowels at the end of a syllable are usually long (even if there is only one letter in a syllable). Long vowels say their own name, so to speak. The third syllable is gram. The consonant g is hard because it is not followed by an i or y. So it represents "guh," the sound you make when you swallow. R represents the sound a lion makes when he ROARS. A is a short vowel because it is not at the end of the syllable, and m represents the sound you make when you pinch your lips together and hum. We also like to say "m steals the a" because the a blends right into the m.

All this parsing may seem ridiculous to those who can read easily, but these techniques are crucial in explaining the principles to a child who struggles to make sense of words. The great thing is that learning the 70 phonograms and the basic spelling rules enables one to enunciate, pronounce, and read far more than the English language.

Criticisms have been made that there are so many rules to break in English that some sight reading is required. You will find that there are many common words that young children do memorize by sight because they have seen them so many times, for example, "the" and "Taco Bell." But the symbols and sounds in English don't break the rules as often as most people like to believe. For instance "the" is pronounced "thuh" before a consonant and "thee" before a vowel. Memorizing "the" as a sight word is only half the job. The words that seem to break phonic rules actually have rules that are less obvious, maybe even coming from the foreign language they originated in. *The Writing Road to Reading* explains the rules for even so-called sight words.

The irony in this whole discussion is that for the student who knows phonics very well, all words eventually become sight words; they will look through the code of symbols right to the abstract meaning and read beyond the squiggles on the page. Decoding skills become so easy for them that they can read difficult passages from authors such as Shakespeare or Melville out loud for the first time and they sound as though they have read all the words many times before. This becomes very obvious while teaching classical or foreign literature to a class of high school students. Some students will still stammer and stutter over decoding new words and others will just "see" the pronunciation. A good grasp of the structure of phonics makes the difference in speed and accuracy for students who correctly pronounce words the first time they are encountered.

TEACH SPELLING RULES
INSTEAD OF SPELLING WORDS

Just as some students seem naturally wired for phonics, some children, often the same ones, seem to be able to just spell. Students who easily figure out auditory sequences are usually pretty good spellers. Spelling is the application of phonics in the context of the rules of syllabication. Good spelling skills enhance good syllabication skills, which in turn lead to proficiency in reading. In other words, mastering spelling rules helps students to quickly decode multisyllable words, which leads to speed and accuracy in reading.

Most students aren't spelling prodigies, however, and require practice in spelling as much as they need it in music or any other skill. Spelling without knowing the rules is hard, almost impossible unless you memorize the sequence of letters in every word. If you can't spell, using dictionaries doesn't help much. So the classical spelling teacher's primary task is to teach the spelling rules used in the 1,000 most commonly used words in English. Fortunately, all of the phonics and spelling rules taught while learning the 1,000-word list will apply to the student's expanding ability to spell all kinds of words.

You can easily find the 1,000 most commonly used words on the Internet, but I suggest you prepare to teach spelling by reading *Spelling Plus* by Susan Anthony. It is an easy read, complements *The Writing Road to Reading* (mentioned earlier), and will help you understand how to teach the spelling rules for the most common English words. *Spelling Plus* offers a good daily spelling plan for students until you have studied *The Writing Road to Reading;* then you will be free to teach spelling from any book or word list.

Modern spelling theories come in two extremes—either correct spelling is disregarded, or so many words in so many lists are memorized for short-term tests that most words are really only surveyed. If the spelling and phonics rules are memorized and applied, students will be better spellers. As classical educators, we're trying to ensure that the basic phonics and spelling rules are learned, confident that the maturing student will be able to apply the rules to an increasingly broader vocabulary.

Spelling Plus is easy to use because the word groups are:

1. listed in groups of 15 from easiest to hardest,
2. shown in cursive for handwriting practice, and
3. arranged by spelling rules.

The lists in *Spelling Plus* have all been created in a sensible order that makes teaching the structure of spelling an easy daily routine. Susan Anthony does a good job of explaining the ins and outs of teaching spelling rules without making it difficult, and explains the interesting history behind spelling. As a busy parent, you don't want to waste time teaching words that aren't commonly used until the students have mastered the 1,000 most commonly used words in English. What's the point of memorizing how to spell "humanitarianism" if your child can't use and spell "their," "there," and "they're" properly? During the summer, I break out the old spelling lists and have my high-schoolers spell them to me again so they can identify any weak areas and work on those spelling rules some more.

If your student struggles through the process of spelling simple words, don't hold back on vocabulary building. Read lots of advanced literature out loud to the student. A strong speaking vocabulary, even if you can't read or write well, signifies intelligence. For example, which student would you like to work with, the one who emails, "I'd like to inquire if you have any employment opportunities," or, "Can I have a job?" All of us are judged by the vocabulary we use. Being trained to use the 1,000 most commonly used words properly is a very easy way for a student who is not or cannot be well educated to be more respected.

NATURAL READERS ALSO
NEED TO KNOW THE BASICS

Natural spellers are generally voracious readers, and spelling rules seem to be unnecessary for them. I am a natural reader and speller. I just can't read enough; it's fun for me. Yet I never studied phonics or spelling rules until my lack of understanding caused me to struggle as I taught my own children to read. I didn't study the rules for punctuation until I was in my forties. Until recently, I could not have properly used that semicolon a few lines back.

Before I started to learn about the classical model, I thought I didn't need to study phonics or punctuation because my teachers and test scores indicated that I could read and write better than most of the other students in my classes. As I delved into the classical world, however, I discovered how much room I had for improvement. Studying the basics of reading has made an enormous difference in my life. Because I have studied elementary phonics and spelling rules, I can read foreign words, scientific terms, and rare words much more quickly. I can use more precise and descriptive words in my writing as my vocabulary expands.

So, even if you have a child who is a talented reader and speller, at least lead him through a crash course in basic phonics, spelling, and punctuation rules. Here's why:

1. Students can strengthen their understanding of why the rules work the way they do.
2. Students can be sure they understand how to apply the rules to new words.
3. Students have an opportunity to identify and strengthen any weak areas.

Once students really can spell the 1,000 most commonly used words in English, move on to using their personal writing and English assignments to learn to spell new vocabulary. Just have your student look up new words in a dictionary and spell them a few times. When my class read Melville's *Billy Budd*, we noticed that he likes to use the word "cynosure." We made it a new vocabulary word this week. It is not a word we will master for a list or a test, but we will be sure to look up the word and use it in our literature discussion. My students would only look up and not master "cynosure" because they are currently memorizing the spelling of hundreds of Latin words. Most romance languages use similar spelling rules to English, and the slight phonetic differences are actually interesting if you already know the English spelling rules.

You can also encourage students to take a basic spelling list and add suffixes or prefixes. Don't neglect homonyms, abbreviations, and frequently misspelled word lists if your child is ready for more challenges. The rules for these kinds of word extensions are well explained in *Spelling Plus*.

So, in summary, before leaving grammar school . . .

- ✓ Everyone should memorize the approximately 70 phonograms and 30 spelling rules;
- ✓ Everyone should master the 1,000 most commonly used words in over 90 percent of English;
- ✓ Everyone should learn to use a dictionary;
- ✓ Better spellers should use their own writing assignments as opportunities to study new words.

The truly classical approach to equipping your students to master spelling rules would be to help them write their own spelling curriculum. Assign the students a weekly phonics or spelling rule, have them make an age-appropriate, ten-word spelling list, and check their work. Then have the students read the spelling rule, the word list, and their spelling sequence into a recording device and develop their own spelling program. This method would also require that your students learn how to use the word processor, recorder, dictionary, and spelling rules. At the same time, they could also earn money creating spelling books with lessons for students who can't spell!

At first these classically based learning skills do take more patience than contemporary classroom methods. That's why it is so important to pick significant grammatical rules to practice and then stick with them until they are mastered. The classical model teaches students to depend on their own minds to retain information and not to rely on outside sources to think for them. If the preparatory work is rigorous, the subsequent studies will be much easier.

READING FOREIGN LANGUAGES

One of the goals of a classical education is to teach students to read books in multiple languages and not just in their mother tongue. Americans are at a natural disadvantage compared to the rest of the world since we don't live in a multilingual society. But the world is shrinking, and it's time for us to join our global neighbors in studying foreign languages. When we teach rigorous phonics rules, students can use their decoding skills not only to decipher English words but also to learn foreign languages.

Parents often ask me if one language should be taught before another or if memorizing one set of conjugations from one language before learning the conjugations from another language will be confusing. There are TV ads for foreign language instruction that have adults saying, "I never thought I could learn a foreign language..." In other countries, such as India and Saudi Arabia, early childhood education is still classical and focuses on stressing the basics of language. So their young students learn three or four languages at a time without confusion.

The mind will sort out the different pronunciations and endings if we spend plenty of time with foreign words. Learning many different things in different ways allows the brain to make comparisons, with the result that we learn even more. It's good practice to let the brain sort out confusion. Modern Americans expect learning to read in a foreign language to be hard, so we make excuses or find some other way to procrastinate rather than just doing the hard work to learn the language. It is work to learn something new. There is no magic. Well maybe . . .

If we can grasp that all languages use symbols to denote words and that these words are organized into predictable sentence patterns, we will find it much easier to learn to read other languages. Of course immersion in a culture is the quickest way to learn a language, or to at least get the accent correct so a native can understand you, but we all can't live everywhere all the time. Fortunately, we have books and audios to help us study. Learning the structure of language will make the entire task of reading foreign languages much easier. I will review the structure of language in the following chapter, on Writing.

READING DIFFICULTIES AND DELAYS

Teaching children to read can require much patience if the student has developmental delays. But don't give up! Even the most resistant reader will reach a stage of physical maturation that allows him to read. Since reading is fundamental to an educated mind, it is worth the time to work with a young student with learning disabilities. Throughout this book, I have assumed your child is average and will become a voracious reader sometime between the ages of eight and eleven. If your child doesn't progress regularly through this age range, I suggest you visit an eye specialist or your family doctor.

My four sons all became avid readers at very different ages. When I was teaching our first two boys to read, it would have helped if someone had reassured me that their reading delays were no one's fault. As a longtime teacher's assistant, my mother-in-law noticed that they weren't reading as well or as early as she would have liked, and I had to agree. But she did notice that they had amazing vocabularies from all the books we read together, so she wasn't too worried. Then it happened. For each boy it was like a switch was turned on the day their eyes and brains caught up with their vocabulary. From then on they easily plowed through books.

One of my favorite moments as the teacher of my children occurred during a power outage. My then seventeen-year-old-son, who began to enjoy reading rather late, lit a bunch of candles, pulled a philosophy book off the shelf, and settled onto a stool to read for the evening. A year before, he never would have done such a thing. And if we hadn't educated classically, I doubt he would have ever chosen a book on philosophy. Don't give up; don't lower your standards; don't say "my child was not meant to be a reader." Just keep reading to them and with them until they read well on their own. Then read together for the joy of it!

TIPS FOR DAILY READING

To naturally increase vocabulary, be sure to introduce your children to a wide range of literature. One of the false impressions books on classical education can give is that every book read should be a historical or literary classic. We want our children to feast on a wide variety of words. So include science fiction and historical novels, books on nature and travel and chemistry, and periodicals like newspapers and magazines. Enjoy graphic novels and dragon fantasies and books on great mythological heroes. Don't feel guilty because you are not following a prescribed plan.

There are some classical curriculums that require literature to be read chronologically, as if the "correct" sequence made it a classical curriculum. I totally disagree. The classical model requires one to start with the grammar one knows and build upon it. If you are most comfortable with American ideals, feel free to read about American heroes and then read about ancient or medieval heroes and compare them to the Americans you are familiar with. We read about American scientists and Renaissance scientists and compare them. We read the ancients and British literature and Christopher Paolini all in the same week. A variety of styles and genres is healthy!

In order to read well, you need to spend lots of time reading. Words need to be savored, laughed at and cried over, wrestled with, and stomped on. They should hit us in the head, knock us off our feet, and spin us around. Words should be the thoughts in our heads that comfort, challenge, sharpen, soften, frighten, and embolden. (Franz Kafka famously said that "a book must be the axe for the frozen sea inside us.")

There is also an art to reading the right way for each book. Most of us read everything like it is a novel because we never expected to read differently. My favorite how-to-read guide is *How to Read Slowly* by James W. Sire. A similar, though more weighty, book is *How to Read a Book* by Mortimer Adler and Charles Van Doren. The irony admitted to by both books' authors is that the people who need to know how to read a book rarely know they don't know how to read a book. Those who are already avid readers tend to read these books and then wonder why everyone doesn't read them. So give them a try; it will make studying easier.

Parents often ask me how I can study so many "how to teach" books. When the boys were young, I read nearby while they played in the creek or on the playground. Reading stories out loud to them every night improved my own reading, speaking, and literature analysis skills. As they got older, I read teaching books in the car while they practiced sports. Sometimes my teacher's book was also their textbook, or we would work through an adult-level book together. I'd read a passage to them, ask if they understood it, to which they normally replied in the negative, and then I'd jump to our white board and teach that concept. Reading and discussing books is just what we do . . . when we are not remodeling or traveling or playing outside.

The type of books we read changes constantly. I have been reading to the boys at night since 1983. I will read to my sons and then to my husband for the rest of my life. I look forward to reading to my grandchildren. Some nights I miss reading aloud because we watch TV or I'm not home, but that doesn't make me feel guilty. By the time my youngest son graduates from high school, I will have read to my boys for almost 10,000 hours. Believe me; we have covered every possible kind of book in that time, from medical and science journals to joke books and magazines. With no planned reading schedule, we just read something someone wants to read. Easy!

To challenge our reading abilities, we read and discuss the Bible every morning and compare it to other forms of literature. We own an out-of-print, multivolume series that has broken the Bible into many sections. Each chapter includes the King James version of scripture accompanied by famous artwork, poetry, and stories interwoven in appropriate places. Each chapter includes maps or photos of the geography mentioned along with images of related archeological artifacts. There are also annotations for historical context.

Not only do we use this time to study the Bible, but the discussion leads us to many different subjects such as philosophy, literature, and math. The study guide inspires amazing conversations, since the book includes questions and analysis of the accompanying artwork and poetry. We love the beauty of the King James language and use concordances when the vocabulary stumps us. At the end of 30 minutes, we have had a rich academic and spiritual lesson while still wearing our pajamas.

Our morning reading really challenges our vocabulary. The rest of the morning is spent reading from easier material as the students work on their lessons and stretch their vocabulary. Later, when they read silently, they will choose books they enjoy. This allows them to increase their reading speed and accuracy. By the time the day ends, they will have read below their reading level and at their reading level, and someone will have read to them beyond their reading level.

We read again at night, and this time we let the younger generation lead. Each child chooses a picture book or a passage from a chapter book to read out loud. Award-winning picture books are delightful to all ages. It's always comical to hear a childhood favorite read as a comedy routine by a teenager, or to see a cherished bedtime favorite bring tears to the eyes of an older child who can now understand that he lives in a troubled world. Then I'll read a favorite book out loud for 20 minutes. Afterward, the boys fall asleep silently reading whatever book they choose.

Reading and discussing literature together is a favorite family pastime. If there were no church to attend, no work to occupy us, or no neighbors to keep up with, we would still feel connected to the world through great books. Every family has their values; classical families spend much time discussing the great ideas of mankind.

BUILDING YOUR VOCABULARY NATURALLY

When you teach a child to put away toys, you use words. When you learn a new language, you use words. You use words when you share a joke with a friend, or when you solve a math problem. As soon as our babies are born, we talk to them because we want them to be drawn to the sound of our words. Every newborn learns her mother tongue because she hears meaningful sounds repeatedly. The brain is designed to take those sounds and organize them into an easy retrieval system.

Helen Keller was able to overcome her disabilities after she realized that everything was tied to a word—an idea she could hold in her mind even if she couldn't hear it spoken. No images, no sounds, no symbols were available to her—only touch. Yet she wrote books that were read around the world and regularly gave speeches before large crowds and to world leaders. No matter how handicapped we are, we think and communicate in words.

As parents, we tend to say the same things repeatedly in the realm of family life, but not in the realm of academics. Parents use words like, "No, hot!" or "Clean your room!" We tend to patiently teach words to our preschoolers until they have acquired a vocabulary sufficient enough for general communication. Then we often approach the broadening of vocabulary as a school assignment rather than just a normal, family activity. We aren't quite as good about saying, "Did you sum your addends?" or, "Have you memorized your irregular verbs?"

Reading as a family allows children to build a rich, expansive vocabulary as they fall in love with stories—whether heroes' adventures or fascinating nonfiction. One of the greatest, most satisfying phrases that parents hear from their children is, "Please, read another chapter!" If parents can teach their children to speak and to walk, which are two of the most difficult things humans learn to do, I know they can be their child's best reading teacher.

A child practices the grammar of reading by learning to

✓ listen,
✓ identify the connection between sounds and letters (phonograms),
✓ identify the connection between ideas and words (spelling rules), and
✓ easily recognize the patterns of well-written sentences.

Reading becomes a pleasure when we can read without stumbling over too many new words on a page. Our eyes learn to dance easily over a page while comprehending the author's meaning if we practice the basics by reading a wide array of literature at a variety of reading levels.

CHAPTER FIVE

WRITING

My children, 7 and 5, are Arabic/English bilinguals. They are in an Arabic medium school in Riyadh and receive 8 hours of French instruction per week. I have noticed that formal grammar rules form an integral part of both Arabic and French instruction at their school and this appears to be the general practice in the Arab world.

—Omar Johnstone, English teacher,
a university in Riyadh, Saudi Arabia

IMITATING GREAT THOUGHTS ON PAPER

Writing is very hard to do well. Writing requires an amazing amount of maturity as one applies abstract thoughts from the mind through the hand onto paper. The art of writing requires an author to take an idea or image from his brain and accurately transport it into another's mind using clear words. Writing is thinking on paper. Since writing skills can be so hard to teach, we can make the mistake of allowing students to spend too much time on creative or free-flow composition and never cultivate writers who can explain how to structure a complex sentence or write a coherent paragraph. Learning the tools of composition allows an author to be both creative and understandable.

While our aim is to teach children to write a brief, interesting essay by the time they leave sixth grade, we need to be more concerned with their ability to structure a sentence correctly and to write a paragraph composed of related sentences. Writing a complete essay is possible for older elementary school children, but the bulk of instruction should relate to the many pre-essay writing skills that are part of the equipment of competent authors.

Children are more willing to do hard things when they know they have achieved something worth doing. They are quick to detect flattery when they are complimented on a piece of writing that they know no one can read because the words are spelled wrong, the thoughts are incomplete, and their ideas are unconnected. Flattery develops at the least an aversion to writing and at the worst a cynicism toward doing things well. Don't falsely praise your students' efforts. Always encourage and then move on to constructive criticism.

As hard as it may be to teach writing, be sincere in your estimations of their abilities and spend the bulk of your instruction on the tools of writing. When the creative impulse arises in their hearts, they will be prepared.

It is never too late to begin with the basics of writing. As an adult, I still get frustrated with my own writing skills. The foundational skills of word usage, proper sentence structure, noun-verb agreement, and placement of prepositional phrases are always basic for students of all ages. So, if you are struggling to teach an older student how to write, start with the same skills you would teach to younger children.

Pre-writing skills include physical activities such as neatness, spacing, and typing, and mechanical activities such as punctuating, capitalizing, and proper positioning of phrases and clauses within sentences. Because writing can be difficult, teachers in frustration may try to loosen the rules by allowing "creative spelling" to replace the practice of spelling rules or to give the children credit for creative stories while ignoring grammatical errors. As I homeschool, I consider which of these three major tasks will be emphasized:

1. Position their bodies properly (sit up straight);
2. hold in mind all the mechanics of writing; or
3. clarify the ideas they want to express.

Only one of these processes can be practiced at a time. Assessing the particular task my students are practicing and then offering constructive criticism that they can actually follow will lead to better writing habits. As young writers become more experienced in practicing these individual tasks, they will begin to naturally combine them.

As a parent, you can help your child learn to sit properly and hold her paper and pencil correctly. Your young child practices sitting still when she colors or draws. The mechanics of writing can initially be taught without thought to posture or expression. For example, the best way to teach verb conjugations to eight-year-olds is to help them write out the endings on a big piece of butcher paper on the floor. Only after a child can sit still and write a mechanically correct sentence should we spend much time on thinking about original things to write. Assessing the processes of writing and providing constructive feedback will prepare children to write down their own thoughts.

HANDWRITING AND COPYING

Through leading many parents through seminars on classical education, I've come to realize that we don't always appreciate the importance of seemingly little things. We don't really spend enough time defining the basics in order to know what or how to teach our children. Handwriting and copying are small things that turn out to be foundational to good writing skills.

In 1995, I taught in a Jamaican Christian mission school for two weeks. When I first walked into the classroom, I was appalled at the assignments given to the first-graders. The six-year-olds sat each morning for about an hour copying, in cursive, a long passage of scripture from the chalkboard. As they did so, the teacher worked individually with a few remedial students. All I could think was, "How boring."

By the end of my stay, I changed my tune as I realized the gift these children were being given.

- All of them could sit quietly for a long time.
- All of them could read every difficult word.
- All of them had memorized lots of scripture.
- All of them had the fine motor skills required to look up at a board and replicate the work on a piece of paper.
- All of them had the hand strength to hold their pencil properly and for a long time.
- All of them had beautiful handwriting.

It seemed like such "busy work" when there were so many more interesting things to cover with the students. By the end of my two weeks teaching in their school, however, I began to see that their methods worked while my methods were the truly fruitless busy work. I've spent the time since pondering their methods and trying to imitate their results, especially as it opened my mind to what other educators meant when they referred to the classical model of education. What I witnessed was an instructional method that has been used throughout history, but was foreign to me. Schools today make too light a matter of little things that actually define the basics.

DON'T MAKE LIGHT OF SMALL THINGS

Let's look at these basics more thoroughly.

All of them could sit quietly for a long time. Teaching children self-control allows them to study and listen and think for longer periods of time. If this is difficult for your child, then his body can be trained to cooperate. If he can sit quietly before a computer or TV, you know he is physically capable of self-control. He may have to be emotionally trained to sit still when he is not engaged by a machine, but you know that he *can* sit quietly. Use your knowledge of his ability and slowly teach him to copy a short article by hand. Begin with five minutes a day and increase the time he spends writing until he is used to sitting still for an appropriate amount of time each day.

All of them could read every word. Reading, copying, and repeating the same small amount of material builds speed and accuracy that quickly moves students to higher levels of literacy.

All of them had memorized lots of literary passages. Copying scripture or poems or songs or speeches is one of the many tools classical educators use to build memorization skills and strengthen our minds.

All of them had the fine motor skills required to look up at a board and replicate the work on a piece of paper. This can be very hard for a young child. Tracking images and reproducing them in another medium requires physical self-control and trains the brain to hold ideas. Controlling our head, eyes, and hands as we simply copy allows us as adults to research words and ideas, compare them to another book, and then follow up by writing in our own notebooks. A researcher is practiced at the art of looking at multiple images and replicating. This skill is essential to forming young minds.

All of them had the hand strength to hold their pencil properly and for a long time. Currently schools employ physical therapists to teach children to strengthen their hands to hold their pencils. Long gone are the days of butter churning and bread kneading that strengthened children's hand, arm, and back muscles.

All of them had beautiful handwriting. Though no longer important for communication since the advent of the keyboard, handwriting practice still teaches students to develop an artistic eye for detail. Handwriting makes it easier for us to notice prefixes, suffixes, punctuation, and other "little" things that make the larger task of writing easier.

Copy work is the tool used to develop all of the skills described above. Art and fine motor control go hand in hand. Anything children can copy beautifully teaches them patience and pride in a job well done.

At the time my eldest boys were older than these young Jamaicans, yet they could do none of these things well. But they sure knew how to have fun! The self-discipline trained into the Jamaican children at that school gave them the basic skills needed for everything else they would ever study in any situation. I was pregnant at the time and knew my next child would be taught the skills I was witnessing. These children were very poor, and had some of the same learning disabilities as children in other places, but no one was catering to their weaknesses. The tasks assigned were simple, thorough, and mastered by each of the children. This is the beauty of mastering the core of knowledge and not rushing to survey everything we can think of in fear of gaps in our children's education.

As I have come to understand the difference between the successes of an education in the past compared to current models, I realized the Jamaican classroom had demonstrated the classical model for me. Our nation's capital spends over $13,000 per student per year to educate the students in Washington, D.C. The Jamaican teachers spent very little money on paper and pencils, yet they were preparing their children well. They had a situation similar to the one-room schoolhouses that were so successful in our nation's past, and they had an expectation that the students would work hard with their minds, paper, and pencil (or chalk and slate). No textbooks or handouts. No computers to make things fun or "relevant." They just had students expecting a teacher to show them how to transfer information from her mind to theirs. Concentrating on the small things had made big results for those six-year-olds.

When discussing copying, penmanship usually comes to mind. The classical model emphasizes the art of beautiful penmanship through cursive. Cursive does away with some of the temporary dyslexia of young children as there are no backward letters in cursive. Since all strokes are written forward in a continuous line, students can't write a letter backward. Our job as classical educators is to teach students to make the effort to be at least neat but preferably to aim higher by teaching them to write beautifully. I truly believe things done well contribute to our freedom. I once handed a copy of the original Declaration of Independence to my children. They couldn't read it because at the time they couldn't read the Spenserian cursive script it had been written in. That was enough motivation for me to teach them cursive.

A PLAN FOR TEACHING WRITING

Copying well-written sentences prepares a student for the harder aspects of writing such as structuring sentences with strong verbs, descriptive nouns, gerunds, varied sentence patterns, and powerful words. We need to help students practice the basics slowly and deliberately so they can develop competent writing tools before they become abstract thinkers. A high school student who can't communicate well and is frustrated may feel compelled to act out when he believes no one is listening to him. I think we would see less violence in high school if young adults could appropriately make their case and express their ideas within a forum that listens. When people are upset they want to be heard. We are designed to communicate, and if we can't articulate our thoughts clearly we often lash out or give up. Elementary students should work more on the grammar of writing—the rules and mechanics—and prepare for the time they really need to say something well.

Let's look at a yearly schedule for teaching writing that changes with the natural growth of children. No child will ever learn in exactly the way described below. I am just trying to demonstrate that there is plenty of time to teach writing well by over-learning the grammar and saving the more creative writing skills for later. I also want to demonstrate that if we would start early and slowly, learning to write would be more enjoyable for the whole family.

Four-year-old children and younger can learn to obey their parents and to love words by being read to.

Five-year-olds can be taught to sit still and draw or color so they learn how to manage their hands and arms at the same time that they control the writing surface and position of their bodies. This is hard for them, and parents need to patiently help!

Six-year-olds can copy words from books and whiteboards onto personal-sized whiteboards or paper. Copying is hard at this age, but it trains the student to take care in her work and to think thoroughly about her task. Writing in a straight line with letters equally proportioned and the page evenly filled is difficult.

Seven-year-olds can learn phonics and spelling rules.

Eight-year-olds can learn to write a complete sentence.

Nine-year-olds can learn to prove a sentence is properly constructed by diagramming.

Ten-year-olds can learn to put correctly written sentences into paragraphs.

Eleven-year-olds can learn to decorate and dress up concise, clear sentences.

Twelve-year-olds can put multiple paragraphs together that form a coherent essay or story while using interesting, beautiful words.

According to the National Assessment of Educational Progress, very few adult Americans can write a coherent, logical paper. We need to help our students over-learn the mechanics of writing basic sentences while in grammar school. Then writing creatively, or forming arguments, or analyzing thoughts will be possible during the rhetoric stage.

Many educators wait until students are able to think dialectically to practice writing, and then they expect too much, not recognizing that the students' grammatical skills aren't developed. A classical educator values the rigor and efficacy of working the same ideas over and over. So from the time children can control a pencil, I recommend they copy a single quality sentence a day. The copied sentence can be the foundational lesson for handwriting, spelling, punctuating, and capitalization in the early grades.

Ask them to answer the following questions so they can become observers of their own work and can correct their own mistakes.

1. Is the sentence written neatly, proportionally, and accurately?

2. Are all the words spelled correctly? Is there a spelling rule that could be reviewed?

3. Are proper nouns capitalized, along with the first letter and any I's? Are end marks (periods, question marks, and exclamation marks) and commas copied? Can the student explain why she capitalized and used end marks?

Drawing an accurate picture with words takes time, just like painting a portrait. Seeing and replicating details carefully make it possible to produce art of good quality. You want your children to be word craftsmen.

As the child matures, the daily sentence can include lessons on replacing common words with more descriptive terms, and changing the sentence structure by adding more complex phrases and clauses. Eventually the daily sentence is used to teach the seven basic sentence patterns (see below), the four purposes of a sentence, and the four structures of a basic sentence. A child who works on improving increasingly difficult sentences from first to sixth grade is not going to have any trouble writing a good paragraph in middle school and a great essay in high school.

Creative writing is not the goal in grammar school; the goal is teaching the mechanics of sentence structure. Musicians learn to play the piano by practicing the same scales as every other musician and then reproducing the songs of the masters like Bach and Beethoven. Learning to write requires developing authors to copy very many good sentences originally composed by someone else. We learn to recognize sentence patterns and structures and purposes by copying well-constructed sentences. You would never tell a student to compose original music until he had practiced the mechanics of an instrument and copied the best music. Let him do the same in writing.

If you can grasp the simplicity and richness of copying good sentences, you will produce good writers. I also call this the "iced tea" approach to teaching writing. I don't have to teach writing. I can just sit on the porch and drink iced tea while the kids do all the work and copy sentences. This is a good thing because I will be tired from teaching them to sit still and I'll need a break before I have to teach them the next skill for their writing toolbox: sentence structure!

DISCOVERING THE CORE

Omar Johnstone, an English teacher in Riyadh (quoted in the epigraph at the beginning of this chapter), describes education in Saudi Arabia:

> By the third grade children can already distinguish verbs from nouns, describe the function and use of adverbs and adjectives, and they know the technical vocabulary of language in both languages. I am teaching English grammar at one of Riyadh's universities. This task is made considerably easier by the students' unfailing knowledge with the Arabic terminology used to describe it. . . . One of the cultural problems of the English-speaking world is that it is cut away from its source, from the common experience of the English-speaking peoples spanning some seven centuries.

For forty years, I had no idea that there was a foundational organization to language that every third-grader learned in early American homes and grammar schools. I knew there were many thousands of words in our language and trillions of ways to combine them, but I didn't know there was a very distinct order, a core of information needed to study languages. Apparently the children in Arab nations are taught the order of language. Why shouldn't our students be as well educated?

I did not learn grammar in primary school, so I had to teach myself. Now that I know the specific terminology and system undergirding the art of language, I can teach my children to learn any language, just as Omar Johnstone teaches his students. As it turns out, learning the grammar allows me to teach anything in the natural world. For example, if I know the classifications of sentences and the eight basic parts of speech, I can write a clear sentence. If I know the four laws of math and the four operations, I can study trigonometry and calculus on my own. If I'm familiar with the constellations, I'm never lost at night.

I have been grappling with teaching languages to myself since 1997 and with English in particular since 2002. When I first began to study foreign languages with my older boys, I realized I didn't know what the texts were referring to because I didn't know the terms used to describe parts of speech in my own language. Verbs have moods? What is a perfect progressive verb? What's a transitive verb? These were among the questions being asked about parts of speech in foreign languages. So I went back to studying English and found out I should be familiar with the same parts of speech and their functions in my mother tongue.

I did not want my own children to struggle as I did. So for the last decade, I've been trying to discover the most crucial aspects of language and placing them into a system of simple tasks that anyone can grasp. Of course, my leads come from the classical model of America's past when all students learned to decline a noun and conjugate a verb and parse a sentence.

I am seeing the fruit of my efforts after seven years of teaching the foundation of English to my two younger boys. (Note that it took seven years, so be patient with your family.) The eldest had to struggle through nominatives and accusatives while studying Latin, but he *could* struggle and succeed. But we're experiencing an unexpected surprise with his younger brother. He just reads Latin, although he doesn't know why he can read it. He's only eleven and isn't quite an abstract thinker, so he can't explain why he can apply English grammar rules to another language; he just does. It's much like those students who can solve a math problem in their head but don't know why. He has very low grades on the Latin tests from the book, but he can translate the Latin into English. I think it is because he has internalized so many ideas about language. So he's like a five-year-old who can read in his native tongue, but can't explain the rules of phonics or grammar.

His low test scores make me curious. I will watch his progress and see what happens on the day when he can explain *why* he can read the Latin words. I still get tangled up in my third-declension words and have to check the sentences he translates with me. He just waits for me to look up the declension and then smiles because he is right every time. I laugh with him and ask, "How'd you do that?"

STRUCTURE OF ENGLISH

There are some languages that are structured differently from English, but they are still all analogous to English. In another language, if the direct object doesn't come after the verb as it does in English, a student can ask, "Well, where does it go?" because she knows it has to go somewhere. If the foreign language studied doesn't use verb tenses in the same way as the romance languages do, she can ask, "Well then, how do you distinguish time and tense in your language?" Maybe they use adverbs as the Chinese do instead of helping verbs and suffixes as in English. The point is that a student can know what questions to ask and can understand the answers if she knows the details of her own language. She can compare the new information to the ideas she is already familiar with. The classical educator teaches students the rules and origins of their mother tongue so they can explore all languages.

Here is the basic structure of English:

1.   There are four sentence structures: simple, compound, complex, and compound-complex. All sentences are either

simple sentences or use conjunctions to combine simple sentences into one of the other three.

2. There are four purposes to a sentence: declarative (use a period), exclamatory (use an exclamation mark), interrogative (use a question mark), and imperative (drop the subject and use a period as in a command).

3. There are seven patterns that form a simple sentence:
   a. Subject–Verb Intransitive
   b. Subject–Verb Transitive–Direct Object
   c. Subject–Verb Linking–Predicate Noun
   d. Subject–Verb Linking–Predicate Adjective
   e. Subject–Verb Transitive–Indirect Object–Direct Object
   f. Subject–Verb Transitive–Direct Object–Object Complement Noun
   g. Subject–Verb Transitive–Direct Object–Object Complement Adjective

4. In English, a complete sentence contains capitalization, punctuation, a subject, a verb, usually a direct object, and forms a complete thought.

5. English words are either nouns, pronouns, verbs, adverbs, conjunctions, interjections, prepositions, or adjectives.

6. Phrases are added to modify one of the parts of speech in a sentence.

These six groups of ideas are the foundation of all language. Sentences are made by mixing and matching these ideas. The rules are beautifully simple and infinitely useful. And, best of all, any child can learn them before the age of twelve. Children who are involved in the daily study of the details of English can apply the same rules to other languages.

The brain power required to attack words is immense, but we know students are wired to learn this way because they can all speak words from a very early age. It's the habit of "daily doing" and the attitude that learning the material is possible that encourages students to keep working. Learning to read and write is the hardest thing humans require of their minds. Mastering language skills enables your child to learn anything. This is why classical educators promote the liberal arts—the liberal arts are truly the arts of a free people.

Now you may find yourself in the position of teaching English grammar to your children, and wondering if learning so much grammar is necessary. Classical educators are convinced that grammar is very useful, but more importantly, it is beautiful. It's hard to know what skills our children will require in the future, so teach them the basics whether they seem immediately useful or not. Maybe one of your children will be a writer and will need these skills. Or maybe your son will need to be equipped to teach writing to a grandchild who wants to become a writer. One purpose of education is to pass knowledge and skills along to the next generation, so even if a basic skill doesn't seem useful to me, maybe I can use it to help another. As an aerospace engineer, I never thought I'd need to learn all the details of language. My schooling was very practical for a single field of study. Who knew that one day I'd be homeschooling, running a curriculum company, publishing books, and traveling as a public speaker? My support network of classical parents is constantly correcting my writing mechanics and word usage. We work together to improve our knowledge as we recover the skills of learning with our families. I rejoice that it is never too late to learn. And it is never too late to learn how to teach.

Commitment is required to make word study a natural part of your home life, especially in this day of parallel monologues when there are multiple talking heads shouting out their opinions on a newscast. Everything won't be easy at first. Have fun learning the material with your child. Be prepared to learn and then unlearn "facts" that are refuted by new information. It shows you can think. For example, you may learn that the sum of the interior angles of a triangle add up to 180 degrees. Then later you learn that it is only true if the triangle is flat or two-dimensional, as on a piece of paper. If you draw a triangle on a sphere like a globe, the angles add up to more than 180 degrees. The fact didn't change as much as the qualification for using the fact.

The classical model can take years to grasp. For writing, especially, it is important to master the art or skill of correct word usage and sentence structure so you have a chance of producing a quality product—that is, something clear and interesting. Concentrate on asking questions and finding answers about writing with your students. Help them to form questions about language so they develop their own interest in the material. Learning the roots of words, the placement of phrases, and the tricks of punctuating can lead to additional questions, turning the writing of sentences into a puzzle that allows us the pleasure of piecing together a beautiful picture rather than struggling with a task we don't really understand.

PUNCTUATION AND CAPITALIZATION

Punctuation and capitalization are easy to teach dialectically. Even though the focus of this book is on grammar, the art of questioning and comparing can be practiced on grammatical rules. "Dialectically" means that the answers should inspire a conversation between the teacher and students as they compare ideas that have been mastered with new concepts. After explaining a hard and fast rule, such as that "dog's is possessive singular but dogs' is possessive plural," ask the student to repeat the rule back to you when he uses this rule improperly in his writing. For example, you can ask, "I see you confused the apostrophe at the end of 'dog'. Do you remember the rule?" When he has a question in his mind, he can apply the memorized rule and begin making the mental connection to its usage. Talk often about punctuation and capitalization. In my experience, students don't do either correctly on a consistent basis until they are about twelve years old. Before that age, when they are writing they are thinking about ideas. After that age, if they have enough experience in copying, capitalization and punctuation become much more automatic while thinking and writing.

There are many rote punctuation and capitalization books. I love them. Use them for practice when you have a busy day or for those days that you spend too much time in the car and need to encourage your children to review basic skills, or for when you've been up all night with the baby and are too tired to really help anyone. Otherwise, teach the rules for punctuation as your students work on editing their daily writing assignments.

When it comes to punctuating, the writer often has a choice. As with everything else in writing, there are rules, and then there is style. Style allows for choices of clarity on the author's part. But my style choices will be better if I understand the rules for usage. For instance, I may choose to put explanatory information in parentheses, or I may choose to make the information part of the story.

> Example: I ate the worm. (I learned to love them while living in the jungle.) It was good!
> *Versus*
> Example: I ate the worm. I learned to love them while living in the jungle. It was good!

Both short paragraphs are punctuated correctly, but change the flow of the story. So if your student chooses a different punctuation than the answer provided in the back of a textbook, put your brains together and pull out a resource such as *Our Mother Tongue* by Nancy Wilson and figure out if and why there might be more than one way to punctuate the sentence. Clarity of meaning is the purpose of punctuation, not obeying rules for rules' sake. There are some different uses of rules in different books by different authors. The rules for each punctuation symbol are close to universal, but there is some flexibility in application. I like *Our Mother Tongue* for beginners and Warriner's *Grammar and Composition* for difficult punctuation questions.

Remember that young children can only work on one new process at a time. If your young students are working on creative writing, punctuation, capitalization, and spelling all at the same time, errors should be expected. This is why we make multiple drafts of a writing assignment. If your students are working on mechanics only, the sentences will be less creative. It is only after they have had a lot of practice in all those areas that the creative skills and the mechanical skills will come together. Be patient and repetitious, and help them approach the same skills from a variety of angles.

Below is a checklist of standard punctuation rules. This checklist—especially the first five rules—if used consistently, will help students with punctuation questions on standardized tests. It is very important for beginning writers to practice often these points of punctuation and capitalization. Inexperienced students should master the first five rules correctly and consistently and then work on the rest.

PUNCTUATION AND CAPITALIZATION CHECKLIST

1. The first letter of every sentence is capitalized.
2. A correct end mark such as a period (.), exclamation point (!), or question mark (?) is always used.
3. "I" as a word is always capitalized. *He and I are happy.*
4. All proper nouns (specific names) are capitalized. *I love Mom.*
5. All other words are lower case. *Children love moms.*
6. All possessive nouns or pronouns end with either ('s) if singular or (s') if plural. "Its" has no apostrophe when possessive. *It's the monster that eats the boys' cat when the girl's monkey opens its cage!*
7. All abbreviations end with a period, except for postal standards. *Mr. Jones, who lives in Troy, NC, ended his letter with a p.s.*
8. All lists are separated by commas. *The big, fat, brown hog ate the swill, the slops, and the cornhusks.* (The commas

separating nouns are known as serial commas: *This, that, and the other.*)

9. All appositives—an additional, identifying noun placed beside an equivalent noun—are surrounded by commas. *I, Jill Pill, gave him, my brother, a dollar bill.*

10. All compound sentences have commas before conjunctions. *Jack and Jill are nice, but I am nicer.*

11. All clauses in complex sentences are separated from the main sentence by commas. *When we play, we have fun. We have fun, sure, when we play. We, who play, have fun.*

12. All speech needs to be surrounded by quotation marks and has the ending punctuation inside the quotation marks. *"We live!" shouted the man. The man shouted, "We live!"* (Note the use of the comma.)

13. All dashes are used to indicate an abrupt break in thought or to set off parenthetical information. *We gave him the right to become president—not to become a dicatator.*

14. Hyphens are used to link compound words, in numbers, and to indicate linkage when a word is broken at the end of a line. *The well-known teacher had forty-two hundred former students at the dinner her friends hosted for her retirement*

15. Semicolons link independent clauses in compound sentences. *We love the beach; we adore the warm sand.*

16. Colons mean "note what follows," or are used to separate hours and minutes when indicating time, and to indicate chapter and verse as in the Bible. *After 3:00, put down your pencil and read the following excerpts: Genesis 2:5–10, and John 3:15–30.*

17. All parentheses are used for information that is related but not absolutely essential to the thought. *Harriet Tubman (1820–1913) led the Underground Railroad.*

PARAGRAPH STRUCTURE

The basics of a paragraph are easier to teach once the idea of a complete sentence has been practiced for many years. Otherwise, students get lost correcting their sentences and forget the topic of the paragraph. I'm an adult and I still struggle line by line with writing paragraphs. Writing is hard, so expect it to take the largest part of your instruction time.

The secret to teaching how to write good paragraphs is the same as that for writing good sentences. Copy. Imitate examples of excellence. Again, students will be able to express their creativity more easily if they first spend time copying good paragraphs. Once students spend about 15 weeks copying paragraphs, they will begin to resist and will want to write their own paragraphs, and the results will be good because the process has been practiced. I tell my students you can work hard at being creative, structuring your paragraph, and checking all the mechanics, or you can do what seems like busy work for a few weeks so that you learn the structure of a paragraph, and then I can set you free to be creative and clear.

When the student is finished copying accurately a paragraph, ask the following questions:

1. What did the first sentence tell you?
2. What did the last sentence tell you?
3. How did the author connect the thoughts from the first sentence to the last sentence?
4. What was the paragraph about?
5. Did you notice the indentation at the beginning of the paragraph? Why is it there?

Once the student can explain that the first sentence introduces the paragraph, the next few sentences clarify the introductory sentence, and the last sentence repeats the main thought in the first sentence, she can actually write a paragraph. This is not how every paragraph has to be written, but it is a good formula for beginners. When the student can identify the main parts and ideas in a paragraph and can construct a coherent paragraph, she can move on to the five-paragraph essay.

Teachers and parents often want students to write long papers before they are really prepared, and then everyone gets frustrated and wants to quit. Work on great sentences and then cohesive paragraphs; essays and reports will eventually follow. Classical educators want writing to be so natural and over-practiced that our students continue to write for a lifetime, not just until they graduate. As you practice the classical model, you will find you can move more quickly than I have described, but be very patient the first few years.

So what exactly do classical educators do to teach how to write besides instructing students to copy sentences and paragraphs? We read a lot of books so the students' "thinking" vocabulary is much larger than their writing vocabulary. And we spend a lot of time teaching children how to copy the ideas of others and put them into their own words. This is how Benjamin Franklin taught himself to write. He would take a well-written passage and write notes on the main ideas and think about what the author was saying. Then he would try to replicate what the author said by only looking at his notes. Once he could replicate the author's thoughts, he would rewrite the passage until he thought his own writing was better than the original. He would use the original passage to correct his faults.

Here's what a classical writing lesson looks like:

We need to have room to wrestle with ideas, and a chair is too confining for the entire process.

Start with copying and improving a single paragraph and graduate to longer passages and then to multiple passages from multiple resources. I found that by the time most students were in eighth grade, they could read an entire book, identify the theme or answer the assigned question, introduce the assignment, write three supporting paragraphs with quotes, and write a concluding paragraph, if I helped them think through key words and an outline.

Sit still and
1.   Read a paragraph from any subject and take notes that reflect the author's key ideas
2.   Talk about the paragraph and notes

Move around and
3.   Go to the whiteboard and together write sentences from the notes
4.   Go over the sentences and replace weak words with strong ideas
5.   Compare your sentences to the original author's ideas, and correct accordingly

Sit back down and
6.   Make a first draft of your sentences
7.   Make a final draft with all mechanical errors corrected

When I first began teaching classical writing seminars, I had to work very hard to get my ninth-grade students to even *try* to write 500 words. It was just too big a challenge and they had little practice. Now 500 words on a subject are not enough for my ninth-grade writing seminar, as they have been trained classically for most of their education. They are assigned two or three papers a week. I have to limit them to reading their best 50 words aloud in class because otherwise we'd just be listening all day. They all want to read and discuss their papers, and I can't blame them. They worked so hard on them.

We've been doing the "50-word readings" for about 10 weeks so far this year, and I noticed this week that their 50 words are rapidly improving. Instead of randomly picking a paragraph to read, they are picking summary paragraphs that present their analysis. When you expect students to copy the great ideas of authors in grammar school, they have no problem producing original thoughts in rhetoric school.

One of my own sons is not an enthusiastic writer, and he plans two hours for each 500-word paper. He doesn't care if he writes well for class, so he puts as little effort into the assignment as possible. He meets with me as he begins his thinking process to be sure he's on the right track. Then he types until he is ready for my "red pen." He makes the final edits and is finished. On the other hand, he is always writing for pleasure, because he likes to put together gaming strategies. So he pleases me by writing short, coherent, analytical assignments and then he's free to write what he likes to write about.

On the other hand, my youngest son, who has been classically educated since birth, literally dances around until he finds the right word for each thought. He's an active little boy and it helps him to move when he thinks. Remember, sitting still and thinking are two separate processes. When he is finished thinking, he sits still and writes. His papers already exhibit a broad vocabulary. At this point, I insist he be quiet when he is thinking, as he processes everything out loud and usually the rest of us are thinking at the same time. But he can spin around on the floor all he likes. I go over his five-paragraph essays one paragraph at a time because at eleven years old he still needs a lot of instruction on the mechanics of writing. He would get upset at all the red marks on five paragraphs, but is undaunted by a single marked-up paragraph.

Imitation is the key to becoming a great author, or a great artist. Imitation is the key to becoming a great anything. You are good at the things you enjoy because you spend time with them, and you look to experts for help, guidance, and inspiration. Consider your own talents as you consider working with your children. Identify the skills and subjects you are comfortable with, evaluate how you became so comfortable, and then use that self-evaluation to help your own children when they struggle. Also, share the academic areas you struggle with and point out that in order to overcome them, you need to work hard. The scariest, yet best part of home-centered education as a parent is knowing our children will imitate us.

CHAPTER SIX

MATH

The chief aim of all investigations of the external world should be to discover the rational order and harmony which has been imposed on it by God and which He revealed to us in the language of mathematics.... Just as the eye was made to see color and the ear to hear sounds, so the human mind was made to understand quantity.

—*Johannes Kepler*

THE CORE OF A CLASSICAL MATH CURRICULUM

A classical math curriculum mandates that students master a core set of math facts. Fortunately, children acquire this core of information regularly and easily when they memorize the multiplication (or times) tables up to ten times ten. As classical educators, we want to teach our children to memorize these tables along with those expected to be memorized by children from early America. Expect your students to also

1. memorize the tables through 20 × 20,
2. quickly multiply and divide double-digit numbers,

3.   memorize the common squares and cubes,
4.   identify the laws in math problems,
5.   add and subtract multiple digits in their heads,
6.   wrestle with ideas about equality, and
7.   have mastered basic forms of numbers.

There are many other concepts they should master, such as shapes, patterns, place value, and measurement. In general, there are three principle ideas associated with every problem:

1.   Numeracy: what kind of numbers are in the problem and how do they work? In arithmetic, students learn about whole numbers, counting numbers, fractions, mixed numbers, decimals, percents, ratios, and scientific notation.
2.   Operations: what mental processes do the symbols represent? Besides addition, subtraction, multiplication, and division, students should be comfortable with exponents and roots.
3.   Laws: which laws of math allow me to manipulate the variables and coefficients and find a solution? The laws of math that children need to practice until they are automatic are the associative property, the commutative property, the distributive property, and the identity.

This basic grammar is often overlooked as students rush to complete a math problem and get a good grade rather than actually studying the explanation and examples while memorizing key terms such as lowest common multiple or reciprocal. If you spend any time with math students, at some point each of them will say, "Just show me how to do the problem." It is all right to learn this way, but not *only* this way. Understanding math algorithms (processes) are as equally important as math answers (artifacts).

The best way to teach the basics is to constantly ask your children to identify why they do a math problem the way they do. They can get very irritated by this method, however, because they just want to follow the algorithm and find the answer. And they can get away with that until about the end of arithmetic studies. Then, suddenly, math gets hard and they don't like it anymore. So ask your children to explain which math laws and operations they are trying to use when they have a question. For example:

$$3.4(2.4 + 5.4) = 3.4(7.8)$$
due to addition and the associative property

and

$3.4(7.8) = 26.52$ due to multiplication.
All the numbers used were decimals.

A fifth-grader can easily do this problem, but he may be challenged to explain why he can do the problem. The classical model for math emphasizes memorizing facts for speed and accuracy, and discussing numeracy, operations, and laws for understanding.

There are plenty of great math curriculums to choose from, but we need to break the habit of working through the book, getting a grade, and moving to the next level. If we are ever going to recover math competency in the United States, we need to slow down and understand math and how it works and why it seems like a foreign language. The rest of the chapter will discuss solutions to things that hinder a rigorous understanding of math and how to overcome our cultural innumeracy. Once you know how to study math, just about any textbook will work just fine. We tend to blame our aversion to math on the teacher, the text, or an innate inability. As with most things we blame, they are not the real culprits. The real problem is that math, like a foreign language, uses unfamiliar symbols, sentence structures, and grammatical rules. So the best way to become fluent in math is to immerse yourself in its language.

RECOVERING COMPUTATION SKILLS

If you read other books on classical education, you may hear that classical educators delay math studies. The quadrivium, which complements and follows the trivium, was based on the study of advanced mathematics. Once the basic skills of grammar, dialectic, and rhetoric were introduced, students were expected to apply these skills to higher-level concepts like music (harmony), astronomy, geometry, and algebra. You can make an argument that classically, the formal study of abstract math concepts were delayed as specializations, but that the grammar and practical application of math was taught naturally at home. If the classically educated students hadn't already mastered basic numeracy and operations, they would never have attempted the quadrivium. Also, our earliest textbooks demonstrate high computational expectations.

Before the 1950s, the standard eighth-grade graduation recitation in America required mastery of the grammar of basic geometry, algebra, and multiple-digit division and multiplication. The information was recited and then demonstrated by a few problems completed on a chalk and slate. Young adults in one-room schoolhouses taught math using very slim texts like *Ray's Arithmetic* or *Euclid's Geometry*. The only calculators present were the brains in the heads of the teacher and students. In a time when every acre, timber, fabric, and ounce was measured for sustenance, people knew math. My family buys everything at the store, so the only math skill we regularly practice is multiplication of percents on sales and discounts. I have to purposefully teach math to my children *from an early age.*

Math seems difficult because it asks us to pack a lot of meaning into unfamiliar, nonalphabetical symbols. I tell my students that mathematicians are lazy (I can say that because I was educated as an engineer, myself), and we want to write as little as possible so we can think as big as possible. For example:

We first learn to count 1, 2, 3, 4, 5, 6, 7, 8, 9.

Then we learn to add 3 + 3 + 3 = 9.

Then we learn to multiply $3 \times 3 = 9$.

Then we learn to use exponents to calculate $3^2 = 9$.

All of the above processes arrive at the number 9, but each time we write fewer symbols and mean more by them. If the preliminary symbols aren't over-practiced to the point of being automatic, our minds come to a complete stop and refuse to progress any further in math until someone sorts out the confusion and helps us discover where we got lost. The mature mathematician can sort out his own confusion.

The main goal of arithmetic, which is the grammar of mathematics, is developing computational skills and memorization of basic laws and formulas. In other words, when I encounter long equations or difficult new concepts, I want the answers to basic operations to be so obvious that my mind can focus on the new application of mathematical laws. You know your high school student has a deficit in basic math skills when he needs a calculator to work out a simple problem from a sixth-grade math text using basic operations like $x = 11^2 + 25^{1/2}$. (The answer is $x = 121 + 5 = 126$.) So whether you begin early math studies with a text or just drill your young children in operations and computation skills (math facts) as you go about your day, be sure that your child is developing his brain's calculator to be quick and accurate.

CALCULATING COMPETENCY
INCULCATES MATH ENJOYMENT

Completing math problems is one of my favorite activities. I like solving mystery novels before I reach the end of the book, and I like solving system problems within business management. When these kinds of solutions are proven true, I feel very satisfied that I was able to think through a puzzle to its conclusion. But these activities take a very long time to complete and satisfaction is delayed. In comparison, in just a few minutes, I can solve a number of math mysteries, check if they are correct, and feel my brain naturally release endorphins of pleasure and satisfaction. As my friend Andrew Pudewa says, "This is helpful for those of us who don't do many drugs." Running through a few math problems with my children provides me with the same satisfaction others receive when they finish their "to do" list.

Every math problem provides a micro-example for practicing the skills of learning. The students demonstrate that they have mastered the math terms used (grammar) and that they understand the rules and strategy of the problem so they can solve the problem (dialectic). Finally, they explain how they solved the problem rhetorically, demonstrating that they understand the algorithm.

Consistent study habits are the most important part of learning math. Grammar school students will proceed much more easily into dialectic, abstract math if their parents help them develop the following habits:

- Work on math lessons as a daily habit.
- Drill and practice for speed and accuracy.
- Move slowly through foundational ideas by over-practicing concepts.
- Demonstrate neatness when writing a problem.
- Learn inverse operations for additional practice and to check answers.
- Learn to create and explain problems to demonstrate competency with a concept.
- Do not permit calculators until trigonometry.
- Copy every problem and each step in order to self-check the work and identify where help may be needed.

The list above instigates a lot of battles between students and teachers, especially among the smartest of immature students. It is easy to calculate arithmetic problems without being neat or writing down steps or even bothering to use a pencil and paper. Of course $2 + 3 + 5$ is 10, and most children can just name the answer without writing anything down. But problems won't remain that easy. As mature adults, we know this to be true, but our students usually don't believe us.

When someone is creating anything, there are two aspects of the creation to consider: the process and the artifact. Just like reading and writing, math is a basic skill because learning the process is as important as obtaining the correct answer. While studying the basic skills of math and writing, we want our students to get a correct answer or write a legible paper (artifacts), but the process of deriving the answer or creating the paper is very important and requires patient effort. Math competency is also related to reading competency because we can't even write or solve a lengthy math problem if we can't read.

So, as a parent who wants her children to love math, I have two duties that are diametrically opposed, yet equally important: to provide plenty of opportunity for mental calculation using only the brain, and to provide plenty of opportunities for paper calculations. This is why we both drill addition, subtraction, multiplication, division, exponents, and roots, *and* we have our children sit down and work through a math text. It can confuse our children. "Which do you want, Mom, for me to do them in my head or to do them on paper?" The answer is not only to do both, but also to know when each approach is appropriate. These skills are analogous to writing in that I want spelling and punctuation over-learned (like math facts) so it just flows out of my children's heads, but I also want them to struggle with clarity in expressing mathematical ideas on paper.

The above discussion once again highlights the difference between contemporary and classical education in that classical educators recognize that the same skills are needed for both writing and math. The basics are always fundamental and worthy of the majority of our children's time in academic instruction.

Today, one of the most popular math textbooks used by elementary schools is the *Everyday Math* series. Instead of teaching students to hold three- and four-digit numbers in their minds while they multiply and carry to find a solution, students are shown how to draw a lattice, insert numbers into the lattice cells, and then add the digits up.

Students are essentially shown how to draw an art project that is inefficient for more than a two-digit-by-two-digit multiplication problem. This presents two problems: first, students need to use a calculator for larger problems, and, second, even engaged parents are intentionally crippled in their ability to help with homework. Parents know how to solve multiplication problems the same way people in the Western world have solved them for 2,500 years. Modern children are shown how to create an art project and then use calculators when computing more than two digits.

The emphasis on computation skills without a calculator has also been replaced by photographs and empathy in thick, modern textbooks.

> In a comparison of a 1973 algebra textbook and a 1998 "contemporary mathematics" textbook, Williamson Evers and Paul Clopton found a dramatic change in topics. In the 1973 book, for example, the index for the letter "F" included "factors, factoring, fallacies, finite decimal, finite set, formulas, fractions, and functions." In the 1998 book, the index listed "families (in poverty data), fast food nutrition data, fat in fast food, feasibility study, feeding tours, ferris wheel, fish, fishing, flags, flight, floor plan, flower beds, food, football, Ford Mustang, franchises, and fund-raising carnival.
>
> —*Diane Ravitch*

In a May 2005 article refuting the current math standards of the National Council of Teachers of Mathematics (NCTM), a group of university math teachers enumerated concern over the following points:

1. Student self-discovery of new concepts is time-consuming compared to a teacher demonstrating and leading understanding.

2. Children who do not master basic operations to the point of automaticity struggle with algebra concepts. "The snubbing or outright omission of the long division algorithm by NCTM-based curricula can be singularly responsible for the mathematical demise of its students. Long division is a pre-skill that all students must master to automaticity for algebra (polynomial long division), pre-calculus (finding roots and asymptotes), and calculus (e.g., integration of rational functions and Laplace transforms). Its demand for estimation and computation skills during the procedure develops number sense and facility with the decimal system of notation as no other single arithmetic operation affords."

3. Even though we want our children to understand why math works and the importance of mathematical concepts, skill mastery precedes abstract application.

    "The starting point for the development of children's creativity and skills should be established concepts and algorithms. . . . Success in mathematics needs to be grounded in well-learned algorithms as well as understanding of the concepts. . . . That students will only remember what they have extensively practiced—and that they will only remember for the long term that which they have practiced in a sustained way over many years—are realities that can't be bypassed."

4. Children with learning disabilities or delays thrive on regular expectations that are increased slightly as skills are mastered. This is the Saxon approach from counting through calculus and physics texts. John Saxon rejected the conceptual, experiential approach and actually emphasized structure and drill. "Large-scale data from California and foreign countries show that children with

learning disabilities do much better in more structured
learning environments."

5. According to a study from Johns Hopkins University,
    there is a strong correlation between early use of calcula-
    tors and poor performance in calculus. And when com-
    pared with foreign countries whose students don't use
    calculators, American students don't do as well.

6. Word problems and contextual problems should be few
    compared to practicing algorithms and operations.

MATH TEXTS

Parents often wonder what math curriculum to use at home. I have used a
wide variety and have found that most of the texts popular among homeschooling families work just fine. Choose an arithmetic curriculum that
emphasizes drills over pretty pictures and social values.

I like to use the book rather than let the book use me. I am not a slave
to the book's lesson plan, but am free to teach my children how to use the
textbook as a reference. In other words, if the lesson has 30 problems, but
we have struggled with a new concept and only get 15 problems completed in the allotted time, I don't feel I have failed my child. The lesson
can be finished the next day. A benefit of homeschooling is the ability to
go at a pace that allows your student to master the material.

On the other hand, if my child completes a lesson or even a text, we
often do the whole thing over again. I *will* fail my child if I move him
ahead in a math book when the fundamentals aren't over-learned. Sometimes we will work through the odd problems together and I'll leave him
to do the even problems on his own.

I *never* let my students skip problems. To me there is no such thing as
knowing math too well or being too fast or too accurate. If a problem set is
too easy, great! Make it a timed test and let the students finish early for the

day. How nice to have an easy day now and then. Just remind them of your leniency the next time the lesson is taking longer to complete. The purpose of a math book is to provide a little daily instruction and a lot of practice problems so that my students become as fast and accurate as possible in calculating and understanding concepts.

I use the Saxon Math series as our children's math spine. By spine, I mean the series of texts they will thoroughly complete in kindergarten through twelfth grade (K–12). Since no textbook is perfect for every child at every stage of development, we often temporarily leave Saxon when it becomes too difficult and use other books to strengthen skills until we can tackle Saxon again. If you use a math series that is not designed to go from K to 12, you risk missing important concepts that may be needed a year or two later. On the other hand, if your kids are math whizzes and you know how to teach all the concepts . . . well, I'd still say be sure you have a good K–12 spine. There is no such thing as too much math practice. Say that repeatedly to your children: There is no such thing as too much math practice.

I like to make the analogy to Tim Tebow or Michael Jordan when discussing math practice. Once they achieved success, did they stop drilling the basics? So, even if your students are math geniuses, drill the basics and remember they are never studying just math; they are learning to control their bodies and minds for extended periods of time while thinking.

PREPARING FOR DIALECTIC PROCESSES

Many teachers say they want their children to understand the math concepts rather than worry about the calculations. Classical educators practice both. Mastering the basic operations supports understanding. In fact, you can't understand the concepts if you don't know the basics.

Below is a typical word problem from a fifth-grade text that illustrates the importance of practicing both process and artifact:

Find the product of the difference of 8 and 5, and the sum of 2 and 3.

Do you realize how abstract the ideas in this problem are for a fifth-grader? It is impossible to solve this word problem if you do not know the definition of sum, difference, and product. The problem needs to be translated even further into symbolic language in order to demonstrate the solution process:

$$(8 - 5) \times (2 + 3)$$

But this is difficult to complete if you are unfamiliar with parentheses and the order of operations. Then, logical processes need to be applied to discover that $3 \times 5 = 15$ is the conclusion. Learning how to solve this arithmetic problem requires that the teacher and the student communicate in the universal language of math. The student will retain the definitions for sum, product, and difference along with the proper logical processes for solving the problem by practicing many similar problems over an extended period of time.

We practice solving basic equations like the one above until they are over-learned so that the following equation may be understood by the student in high school:

Find the product of the difference of $8(z + y)$ and $5(z + y)$,
and the sum of $2(z + y)$ and $3(z + y)$.

If this second problem seems difficult, it is because you don't really understand the seemingly simple operations of adding, subtracting, and multiplying. The problem above only requires that you add, subtract, and multiply to solve. We think we understand basic operations; then we discover we haven't even begun to learn how to add and subtract when we encounter algebra. We blame algebra—instead of the real culprits, the basic operations that we didn't learn thoroughly enough—and conclude that algebra is hard. Actually, the basic operations are complex and need more attention so that algebra skills are manageable. Arithmetic is the basic language of math. It requires a lot more practice than most of us realize before we can be fluent in translating basic operations practiced in simple problems into more difficult problems. Here is the answer to the problem above:

$$3(z + y) \times 5(z + y) = 15(z + y)^2$$

which is very similar in form to the previous problem

$$3 \times 5 = 15$$

Algebra is just the application of arithmetic. Our goal in teaching arithmetic is to make basic operations so easy that they aren't even thought about (automaticity) while the student is working hard on the more difficult algebraic concepts.

In order to explain the equations above, a number of language skills were needed. I assumed that you can make the connection between the word "sum" and a plus (+) symbol. I also assumed you knew the basic rules for the operations of adding, subtracting, and multiplying. As a teacher, I have to know the math language and operational processes well enough to explain them to someone who may not know them.

How do I know if I succeeded? My student will be able to demonstrate her understanding by explaining a similar problem to me both in words and on paper. If she can't explain a concept or problem to me, I may need to spend more time teaching her the concept that she is struggling over. I may need to use different words or symbols—language—to explain it another way or with a different example. In either case, understanding math requires that the teacher and student use the proper words and symbols.

Students learning math need to use the same skills they use for learning Spanish or writing. They need to be shown the basic vocabulary and rules of structure and then be led to practice these basics until they are second nature.

Instead, the average student moves too quickly to more abstract problems before understanding the actual operations. Understanding requires more mental maturity and agility than memorizing math facts, but mental agility is initiated by memorizing. Memorizing math facts facilitates the understanding of math operations. Students need to be taught to memorize math facts first, and then to illustrate that they understand the algorithms and concepts by writing out every step.

I feel that I am slightly misleading you, because all learning is really cyclical. In fact, the word "encyclopedia" really refers to the way we learn. Moderns think the word means a series of books with topics organized alphabetically. Classically, it actually means to gather knowledge by going around and revisiting knowledge. According to the *Oxford English Dictionary,* "encyclical education," is "the circle of arts and sciences considered by the Greeks as essential to a liberal education." Every time we cycle through information already learned, we are encountering the information with a different brain than the time before. Old grammar is mastered and then dialectically compared to new thoughts, and then the new thoughts become old thoughts and can be compared to the next thought. While thinking about old grammar, new grammar is being integrated into the brain's memory. So students will move forward in their understanding of addition and subtraction applications while still memorizing multiplication tables. The point is that when a student is just stuck and can't see his way through to understanding a concept, it is usually because something simpler is being overlooked or hasn't been mastered. Developing a core of grammar prepares the student to compare thoughts and think dialectically.

Here is an essay I wrote a few years ago describing a specific math lesson with my young sons. I wrote the math lesson description in 2006. Now, in 2009, those same boys are still using Saxon, still rarely ask questions or need help, and still laugh out loud at the problems. My William, at thirteen, constantly finds applications across the curriculum as he studies

A REAL HOUR OF MATH HOMEWORK

I like Saxon Math texts because they launch our family into so many daily discussions which contribute to our love for learning at home. The authors of the Saxon series have gone out of their way to incorporate both silly and culturally varied word problems along with very serious and even patriotic applications.

For instance, 10-year-old William had a word problem in Saxon about burros. He asked, "What's that?" and I responded with "Another name for donkeys." Then he said, "There are so many names for donkeys—asses, burros..." which gave him a brief synonym lesson and a chance to say a "bad" word without getting corrected.

I was concerned that he would confuse the Spanish spelling with the English word "burrows," so we had a brief spelling lesson. I pointed out that "burro" is Spanish, but "burrow" is English and requires a "w." They both end with the long "o" sound but use two common rules for spelling "o" and "ow." (In "burro," we use the rule that an ending vowel is often long. In "burrows," the "w" acts as a vowel, as in "when two vowels do the walking the first one does the talking and says its name.") The above conversation only caused a minute interruption from our assignments. I sit at the table and write while the boys work on their assignments, so this conversation also took place while 8-year-old David was listening.

As William proceeded with his lesson, David needed my help drawing multiple triangles to measure and count inside of larger shapes. David delights in any new math material. Both boys are able to delight in new ideas rather than feel trepidation at a new math concept because they have been trained to rework problems ad nauseum at grade level and even below. I want old concepts mastered, which means they come quickly and easily to my students. I want new concepts to be a delightful challenge. Saxon's incremental process allows this to occur daily. David has been through two additional math texts for second-graders already this year. These books, which emphasize drills, prepared him to complete about five Saxon math lessons an hour, including breaks for kisses and hugs.

He just asked me, "What does vertical mean again?" I said, "You tell me." He said, "Up and down?" and I said, "Good," and kept typing. Then he interrupted me to help him do his first Venn diagram. William looked over from his side of the table and said, "Oh! Those are fun. They're easy!" So I stepped David through his first Venn diagram. There is another Venn diagram on the next page for him to try on his own. If he can't do it well, I'll help again. If he can, I get to shower him with praise. . . . The verdict is in: he correctly solved the problem and gave me lots of kisses when I said, "Good job!" Now he wants to skip the rest of the problems and do a bunch of Venn diagrams. I said, "No, do all the problems on the page."

Am I squashing his delight in Venn diagrams? Maybe; but I already shared in his joyful math kisses and it's time to get back to work. An important job as a parent is to remind him to get back to work after the celebration. If I have to teach him Venn diagrams tomorrow, it means today's success was only in his short-term memory.

Meanwhile, William is working almost exclusively on fractions today, even though they are presented in a variety of forms in a Saxon lesson. In other words, if you looked at the lesson page, it's not obvious that most of the lesson is on fractions because of the various symbols, words, and graphics on the page. It doesn't look like a fraction worksheet. He isn't required to work on a single pattern that looks exactly the same; instead, he has to stretch his brain constantly and repeatedly apply the process of multiplying fractions in different contexts and forms. To learn, he is processing out loud anything that seems new to him. He tells me his steps and the numbers and answers. I just keep typing away and don't really pay attention. If there is a pause in his voice like he's thinking or unsure, I look up and offer help since I'm aware he is struggling. He doesn't need my input as much as he needs a face to talk to so he can think things through. If my boys feel confident about a concept, there are plenty of practice problems in Saxon. If they are not confident, I make up some problems at the board with them. If that is not enough, I pull out another math text and find a page with similar problems.

Now, William is finished with his Saxon lesson and is checking it himself. He marks the problems that are wrong and recalculates the answer. One time he actually found a wrong answer in Saxon yesterday. The text had switched a divisor and dividend so the answer key had an inconsistent answer. William could not correct his problem and come up with their answer, so he called me for help. I was confused for a moment because the answer key is so rarely wrong. So we called in the "big guns"—Dad. He figured out what had happened. It was a two-part answer, and both answers were correct if two numbers in the original problem were switched.

This situation reveals the various levels of understanding math. William is trying to memorize and use the rules. I could find the right answer consistent with the text's data. But my husband could think through to the author's intent and the lesson being taught to evaluate why the error occurred in the first place. William and I hope to understand math one day as well as Dad.

William is "behind" in math, as he is working through the text for the second time. He just had too many problems wrong the first time through the text, and he had a hard time correcting them on his own. This time through, if he gets something wrong, he can usually figure out why it is wrong. He is mentally maturing from just finding the answer to understanding the concept. Words are easy for William. Math is a foreign language. So, we are tackling math as verbally as possible for him so he can use the tools he knows well—word and definition analysis—to apply to what he doesn't know well, mathematical patterns.

I am not naturally good at math patterns either. Accuracy is very difficult for me, but if I slow down I don't make as many careless errors. I work on math so much that other folks think math is easy for me because I can explain the foundational concepts so many different ways. It's not. It is easy for my husband, as he takes the time to both understand concepts and double-check his computations.

David is naturally good at math, yet I won't let him move ahead too quickly. There are many basic skills to practice besides understanding concepts. David will be permitted to accelerate his progress through texts after he is mature enough to write down every step of every problem, sit still for a whole hour, and check his own work. These are crucial skills that would get missed if I let him move forward with just his strengths. His natural strengths will stay strong. As his parent, I need to help him develop the discipline needed to strengthen weaker areas, which will then allow his strengths to soar! So we over-practice easy problems because we really aren't studying math; we're using math problems to practice study skills and brain training.

We also use Saxon math for part of David's daily reading lesson. The words are above average grade level; for instance, "oblique" and "vertical" aren't typical second-grade spelling words or vocabulary. Yet thanks to Saxon, we read a few new words like that every day, and master their meanings by applying them to math problems.

David also loves the problems. He ended his lesson today by shoving his way onto my lap and saying, "Mom, listen to this funny problem." It was a logic problem about some crazily decorated socks. It really wasn't funny, but somehow all those silly socks delighted my eight-year-old son. Sharing a laugh over a math problem delighted me.

Latin and logic, physical science and the history of science, and has entered the world of earning a paycheck. He has learned to ask, "Who uses this math?" instead of the more common reaction of, "Why do I have to learn this?"

My David, at ten, made my heart sing this February when he told me he was going to start his math book all over again. He was almost finished with it and felt he was just making too many careless errors. Since we work on math every day, just as we read every day, he can get through a couple of math texts a year. Completing the math book isn't his goal. Getting math over with isn't his goal. He decided without consulting his parents that he should just be good at math.

David had Venn diagrams again today in his math lesson, just as he did three years ago. The assignment asked him to apply Venn diagrams to a geometry concept. He needed my help, demonstrating to me, once again, that it takes years of seeing the same thing used in different ways before it can be mastered. If someone asked me before yesterday, "Does David know how to use Venn diagrams?" I would have said "Yes," and been partly wrong. I need to remember he still thinks concretely—after all, he is a child—and I should have said, "Yes, for the types of problems he has previously encountered." Once he is an older, abstract thinker, I will have done my job if I can answer, "Yes, he can apply Venn diagrams to any type of problem." For now, I just have to be patient as he develops his dialectic skills.

CALCULATOR CONTROVERSY

In a past math seminar, I had a student who was just happy to admit that she was awful at math and did not do as well as she could have because she disliked it so much. She and her mother and father and siblings and I all did our best to push or pull her through high school algebra. She ended up going on full scholarship to a selective private school that required students to take college algebra. I could just hear her loud groan and see her rolling her eyes when she first heard the news.

A few weeks into her math course, she called me to share the following story. She had handed in her graphing assignment and the teacher soon gave it back to her and told her she forgot to hand in her calculator strip. She asked, "What's a calculator strip?" The teacher explained that he wanted the strip from her TI calculator that showed her how to graph the answers. She explained that she didn't own a graphing calculator and that she had done all the problems and graphs with paper and pencil. The teacher didn't believe she had done them without a graphing calculator, and she called me to share her outrage.

As Kepler declared in the epigraph at the beginning of this chapter, the mind was designed to understand quantity. Imagine what this student could have done if she had changed her attitude and actually tried to like math! It is good to expect much even from those who claim to hate math, to believe they can learn even when they don't believe it themselves. For, like Kepler, they may one day see that there is harmony and order to the universe and that their minds were created to appreciate the quantities that describe the natural world.

CHAPTER SEVEN

GEOGRAPHY

According to the National Geographic Survey published in May 2006, only half of our students study any geography before graduating from high school, and even among those, only about one-third of young adults aged 18 to 24 can find on a map places affected by recent events, such as the wars in Iraq and Afghanistan, or the floods in New Orleans and in Indonesia. The report tries to make things sound better than they are by repeatedly highlighting as positive the fact than most students now have access to geographical maps and news through the Internet. As classical educators, we know that *access* to information hasn't raised the number of students who choose to spend time pursuing that knowledge. In fact, access to information has only translated into more time chatting with peers and less time with novels and maps and reference books.

Studying geography is actually one subject that is easy to make fun and informative from an early age while working on the basics. It is easy to teach well, as it can engage the minds of all ages and learning styles, yet geography is another neglected subject in American education. Having a basic map in our heads helps us to form accurate images of international conflicts or relive adventures with historical heroes or sympathize with the plights of man beset by natural disasters.

Knowing geography gives structure to real stories. It's hard to get lost in the snow in the Sahara, though one can freeze to death there. It's hard to climb the Great Plains, but you do have to scale some elevation to get to them. It's easier to be charitable when you can empathize with another's economic or ecological conditions. It's easier to be politically astute when real wars are fought in places that are relevant to you.

I am in Patna, Bihar, India, as I write these words. What do you know about Patna? Can you see it on a map in your mind or do you have to look it up? If you can already see it in your mind, you can more greatly appreciate the fact that it was the most populated city in the entire world before 400 BC. Otherwise, you are more likely to pass by this fascinating piece of information because your mind has no context to hang it on. You should be able to ask, "Really? Patna's in the middle of India, and India is a peninsula cut off by the Himalayas. How did everybody get there?" There are interesting mysteries to solve for those who can accurately connect history to a physical location.

According to *National Geographic,* too many of us can't accurately imagine where the subcontinent of India is, let alone picture the location of one of its historically important states. But then, there are innumerable villages, towns, lakes, rivers, and mountains in India. How do we decide which locations to study? The modern answer is to say there are too many, so we'll just teach our students to look them up. Well, I want my kids to have the skills to use atlases and globes for research, too, but not every time they encounter the name of a location in a book or movie or conversation. That makes the process of reading either too slow, or they don't even bother to look up the location at all and miss out on interesting information. Knowledge breeds further curiosity and interest.

The first step to restoring geography education is to teach students to memorize maps. That may sound boring unless you realize how relaxing drawing and coloring can be. Wait, did I just say "drawing and coloring"? Yes! For students new to geography, they should really start out with cartography, the art of drawing maps. Once again, restoring classical education efficiently "kills two birds with one stone." Students can practice drawing maps while listening to classical music or talking to a family member who is drawing and memorizing a map with them.

Just copying maps seems too easy an answer to some. Don't we need to study the culture and government and religion of the regions? Sure, eventually, but having a good world map stored in your head will make all of the aspects of geography easier to place in context later as they are learned, and drawing and coloring maps is an easy place for children to start.

To others, just copying maps seems like too hard an answer. They feel that they could never accurately draw a map of the world from memory. Good education sets the bar high while giving students the practical tools to complete a goal. Until the 1950s, all children drew maps to study geography. The current generation of adults wasn't required to draw maps in school, so we don't understand how useful a skill it is. Or we think it is just too hard for an elementary student to patiently copy large amounts of information. We grew up in the age of the photocopier, so we forget that previously all students used to copy maps for geography.

Usually students are told they are learning geography if they are asked to fill in the blanks on maps whose outlines have already been drawn for them. Too easy! No brain strain required, so students only retain the information in their short-term memory for exams. Repeatedly drawing maps with your own hand develops so many different paths through the brain that it is easier to recall the location later.

So here is how to begin. This plan works as long as the student is at least five years old. Thirty-three-year-olds tend to enjoy it the most.

Find a good world map in an atlas or from the Internet that is 8½" × 11" and has clear lines for the five great circles and outlines of the seven continents. (The five great circles are the latitudinal lines of the Arctic, the

Tropic of Cancer, the Equator, the Tropic of Capricorn, and the Antarctic.) Keep this map handy for a long time.

The grid provided below is a good place to begin as the Great Circles are proportionately drawn. Your goal is to be able to sketch a world map accurately on the grid. Our family enlarged it to 11" × 17" and made a hundred copies. This will give us plenty of practice.

		Arctic Circle
		Tropic of Cancer
		Equator
		Tropic of Capricorn
		Antarctic Circle

I know this doesn't sound like rigorous academics, but I promise you that it is, especially for children. Here's a short list of some of the skills they have been working on:

1. Sitting still
2. Holding a pencil properly
3. Drawing straight lines without a ruler
4. Folding paper

LESSON 1: LABEL THE GREAT CIRCLES

If you want to be very classical and use no copying machines, you can make your own grid by following these directions.

1. Fold an 8½" × 11" paper in half lengthwise (landscape) and then draw a line down the crease. (Teachers call this fold the "hotdog bun" instead of the "hamburger bun," since the fold is on the long side of the paper.) This is your equator.

2. Line the piece of paper up with the atlas so the atlas's equator and your paper's equator make one long line. Looking at the atlas, extend the other four great circles across your paper. Now you should have five lines drawn across your paper that are proportional to the atlas that you want to use. These lines are your Great Circles. Label them from top to bottom just like the atlas. I let the younger students label the lines Ar, TC, E, TCp, and Ant as they say the name of the circles. Older students should write Arctic, Tropic of Cancer, Equator, Tropic of Capricorn, and Antarctic.

3. Draw the Great Circles again on the back side of the paper for additional practice, and then Lesson 1 is completed. Learning how to draw the Great Circles will help us to fill in the rest of the world map, as they will be our best reference points.

LESSON 2: PRACTICING LESSON 1

Repeat Lesson 1 until it is too easy. This is another way to restore education: teach students to do something until they can do it in their sleep.

LESSON 3: THE PRIME MERIDIAN AND INTERNATIONAL DATE LINE

Draw and label the Five Great Circles again. These horizontal lines are called lines of latitude. (Think "laddertude" because you could climb up them like a ladder from the South Pole to the North Pole.) Now we will add a line of longitude (vertical). Draw a straight line down the middle of the page and label it the Prime Meridian (P.M. for little guys and gals).

Now this only works if the world map you chose to copy has the Prime Meridian down the center. The Prime Meridian goes through England and western Africa. If the map you're copying has it somewhere else, you need to adjust the spacing of the continents proportionally. You now have created the grid you will use to draw the continents.

There are maps with Europe in the middle (including the Prime Meridian) and other maps with the Americas in the middle. I'll bet Asians have a map with their continent in the center. This shouldn't matter since the world is actually round. Just be aware that the Prime Meridian is a good reference for a line of longitude (lines drawn up and down, or vertically). That reminds me of another skill that geography forces us to practice: transposing a three-dimensional shape (the globe) onto a two-dimensional shape (map).

If you are confused, just put your Prime Meridian where the map you are copying has it labeled. I know that visualizing these instructions may be hard without a video. That's why we need to restore classical education. Thinking about hard things like lines on maps that aren't exactly where you thought they'd be throws us off balance. If we didn't pay enough attention in geometry class, transposing lines seems difficult. Ignore the Prime Meridian for now if it doesn't help you. You'll figure out where to place it eventually.

On the opposite side of the world is the International Date Line. This line runs between Alaska and Russia down through the Pacific Ocean. If you drew a map with the International Date Line down the center, Asia would be on the left side and the Americas on the right side of the map. There is nothing wrong with drawing a map this way, but since we commonly call the Americas the Western Hemisphere, it makes more sense to have the Americas on the western or left side of the map and use the Prime Meridian as our vertical reference point.

LESSON 4: LEARNING IS SATISFYING

Okay, I know you are a busy adult, but I am telling you, for Lesson 4 get the family together, put on some classical music or an audiobook, get some colored pencils and plenty of plain white paper, and you will be amazed at how fun this is to do. We could have "map parties" like Tupperware parties. The ladies could all get together, draw and eat, and purchase overpriced maps so their hostess can win lots of prizes—such as flags from every nation, or a trip to Aruba.

Try copying maps, any maps, while sitting on a screened porch in the spring. You may revel in the delight of knowing that the world is well made as you recreate it with your students. Learning to learn is satisfying.

LESSON 5: ADDING AFRICA

This lesson gets a little harder for younger kids, so here we accept what I call drawings of continental blobs. The goal is to help the student draw the continents proportionally. Start with Africa because it is in the center of the map and it will help you get the rest of the continents drawn proportionally. Look at the world map in your atlas and notice how long the outline of the continent of Africa is. Does it start above or below the Tropic of Cancer? Does it go past the Tropic of Capricorn? Does it extend farther east than Europe? Farther west than Europe? Does it run into Australia? Does it share space with the Prime Meridian? These questions asked and answered out loud will help your students observe where the continent of Africa lies on the grid of Great Circles. Now draw a blob on your paper that shows about where Africa lies on the globe. No perfection needed. Just draw the general outline of Africa.

LESSON 6: REPEAT LESSON 5

You're probably not happy with the map you drew in Lesson 5. As soon as you drew your blob, you probably knew you drew something wrong. That's okay. Draw the blob for Africa's outline over again on the same piece of paper. This is practice. You're going to throw the paper away anyway, so just draw the outline of Africa as a blob three or four times on top of itself. Draw the map again on the reverse side of the paper (let's not waste paper). Then throw the paper away.

LESSON 7: CONTINENTAL BLOBS

Now get a clean sheet of paper and draw your grid of Great Circles. Then draw your "blob of Africa." Now draw blobs that approximate all the continents. Remember, the goal is to just see how they lie in proportion to one another on your grid. Don't worry about connecting Asia to Europe. Just give them each their own blob. This is supposed to be easy and makes you pay attention to where the continents sit on the Great Circles and in relationship to one another. The main skill learned in this series of lessons is how to look at something very well and replicate its outline proportionally.

LESSON 8: LABEL THE OCEANS

Draw Lesson 7 again, only this time label the continents and the Atlantic, Pacific, Indian, and Arctic Oceans.

LESSON 9: BLOB PERFECTION

Practice your continental blobs until you get them to cross your Great Circles in a fairly accurate manner, or until you are satisfied.

LESSON 10: FINAL PROJECT

Draw your grid of Great Circles and the continents and label them and the oceans as neatly and as well as you can without looking at the original map. Now look at the original, and correct any errors. Repeat until you are satisfied. The example below shows how to begin in a very simple manner, yet convey some good basic information. Even though a five-year-old can draw these grid lines and blobs, very few adults could describe or sketch where the continents sit in relation to the Great Circles.

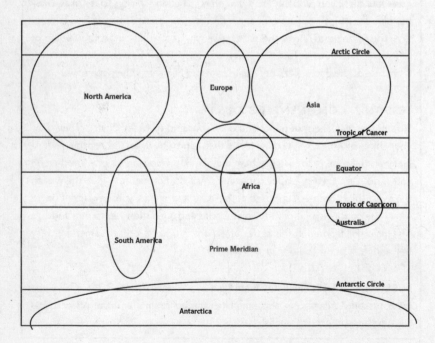

5. Listening to good music
6. Seeing the details on a map
7. Memorizing the Great Circles
8. Memorizing the continents
9. Memorizing the oceans
10. Spending time with their family
11. Aligning vertical and horizontal lines
12. Looking at one resource and copying information onto another (the sheet of paper)
13. Transposing 3-D images to 2-D

Adults make light of these skills because we take them for granted. For children, they have to practice "looking" from one paper to another, or tracking information with their eyes as they move their heads. They have to practice holding a paper still while writing. They have to practice spelling Antarctica. On the other hand, how many adults do you know who can sketch a world map proportionally and label the continents and oceans?

This simple skill will transform your ability to read, think, and participate as a global citizen. It has never been more important to know our globe than today when international trade agreements and United Nations resolutions affect so many of us. Most of us can't accurately place the continents, let alone locate an ancient city-state like Bihar, India. That's silly, especially after we see how easy it is to draw maps and recognize that there are only seven continents—and they haven't moved in the thousands of years man has been making maps. Classical educators want to equip children to feel at home anywhere on their planet.

The magic of these short lessons is the satisfaction the student receives after patiently copying a map. It just isn't that hard to do, but it does take time once they are drawing detailed maps well. Included here is

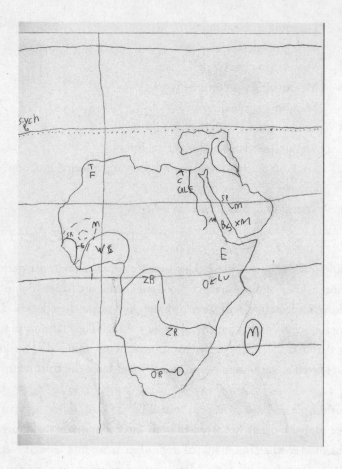

an example of a simple drawing of Africa done by an eight-year-old. Notice his grid, the basic outlines, a few physical features, and that the initials of the features' names are included. It takes him too long to write out
the names of the locations, they are hard to spell for an eight-year-old,
and the initials are enough to remind him of the names of the places. He
is studying geography and mapmaking. Once this is easy, we can work on

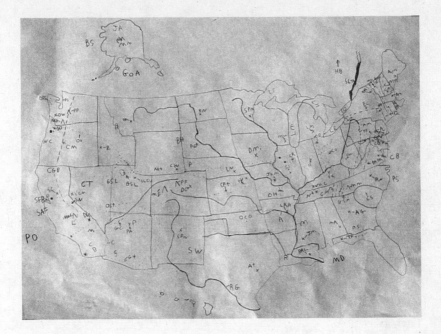

spelling the locations properly. At first, I just want him to memorize the names of the locations.

If drawing a world map still sounds too hard, look at the example of a map of the United States drawn freehand by a ten-year-old. He likes drawing and is good at it because he practices. He puts time into it. He does the same thing over and over again. Above is a map he drew freehand while looking at an atlas. He practiced drawing the map once a day for an entire semester. He started out by tracing and then copying and then drawing freehand. He is currently spending a year mastering the seven continents so he can replicate them in detail on a world map. He has advanced far from a grid with blobs, but continental blobs are where he began when he was five years old. If he can do it, your students can, too.

So, now that we see the possibilities, let's move on. I'm not going to go into as much detail for the rest of the geography lessons, because you actually learned the skill needed for memorizing the world already in the first ten lessons. You just need to apply the skill of observing the proportions on an original map and think about them as you transpose the map's outline onto an empty grid. Eventually it can be done with more and more detailed maps, such as the United States, the countries of North or South America, or Europe or Asia, or the counties within your state, and so on.

Now that you can draw the major features of the world proportionally on a grid, let's tackle the details of each continent one at a time. I like to start with South America. It has a nice easy shape, and only thirteen countries.

We'll use the same procedure already outlined.

Repeat this process for each of the continents. This could take a month of half-hour daily lessons for a teenager, or seven years of weekly lessons if the child starts as a five-year-old. The final goal is to draw the world by heart (from memory) with at least two hundred features accurately labeled.

The more you draw maps, the easier it will be to remember facts, such as that Asian elephants have smaller ears than the African variety because the elephants' homes will pop into your students' minds.

As you become more skilled at drawing all seven continents on one map, you have to ask an important question. Did you draw every place possible? No, of course not, but I'll bet the next time a newscaster reports on a war or disaster south of northern Mongolia or east of western Brazil, a map will unfold in your head and you will have a very easy time placing the news story in context. Now when you look up unfamiliar places, you will be more likely to remember it the next time you hear the place mentioned.

If you're convinced that your students should draw maps, here's an easy-to-follow plan: Once a week draw and label these maps. Another time each week, review the maps the students drew while younger.

Kindergarten: Great Circle grid and continental blobs
First grade: Australia

1. Find a good 8½ × 11″ map of South America with the Great Circles indicated on the map.

2. Draw the great circles that cross South America on your paper, held in portrait orientation (with narrow edge at top), so that they match up with the map. Now you have your grid.

3. Practice drawing the outline of South America as accurately as your age and skill allow. Perfection is not needed. Just try!

4. Once you have a decent outline, start sketching in the borders of the countries. Again, you are teaching your student to "see" where countries lie within their continents around the world. Talk to your students about where the boundary lines begin, how they curve (often shaped by rivers), and where the lines end as you sketch the countries' boundaries.

5. When you're happy with the boundaries, label the countries.

6. Try drawing the whole thing from memory. Correct any errors and work on this process until a friend who knows geography could say to you "Hey! That's a good South America."

7. Go to a map of South America and find ten physical features. Rivers, mountains, lakes, whatever you fancy, and sketch them as accurately as you'd like on your map.

8. Once you can draw the outline, the countries, and ten features from memory, just practice while looking at the original for accuracy.

9. Now add the capitals of the thirteen countries.

10. Finally, frame your best drawing of South America.

Second grade: South America
Third grade: Africa
Fourth grade: North America
Fifth grade: Europe
Sixth grade: Asia

Seventh grade: World map
Eighth grade: Indonesia and Antarctica

For parents and teachers who are worried because their children are older, try one continent per semester. If you are an adult or high school student, try drawing a continent for two weeks each and you'll be done in a semester. The world map probably won't be mastered for life, unless you remember to sketch a world map every now and then for review. Just think: instead of doodling when you're bored, you can review your world map.

There are some ground rules to making maps stick for a lifetime.

1. No premade maps that you fill in—use only your mind, an atlas, paper, and a pencil
2. Lots of practice
3. No perfectionism is required—just sketch until it is easy to see the continent. Work on accurately drawing one line at a time. If you make yourself do the whole map accurately at once, you'll get frustrated.
4. Remind yourself to enjoy the time by listening to music or a book on tape. It takes time till you are good at the details, so make the time pleasant.

What about all the other geography that students can study, such as religious, cultural, environmental, manufacturing, and economic maps? Once you have the political boundaries and major physical features down pat, the other ideas have a place to live. Make the locations of the world's religions or indications of wheat harvest or GNP something else you label on your map if you want. The sky's the limit now that you have a tool to use and label.

And this is the crux to restoring education. Current educational methods disdain memorizing content since it can be looked up, but then require *no* content to be mastered. Our students are never required to master the tools of geography or math or any subject, so no one is educated at all. The so-called rote content is just the material that enables the skills to be mastered. An educated person possesses academic skills because he practiced the processes repeatedly on excellent content. Learning rich, substantive information is a great bonus!

If you are in a classroom setting, it is beneficial to have both a large world map on the wall and a good globe. Use these tools to double-check geographical details as they come up in other coursework. If the world map is large enough, you could use it for the exercises I just described. A large number of students could sit at their desks and look up at the map as they draw it on their blank sheets of paper. Looking up and then back down and replicating something that is large to something that is proportionally smaller is a difficult skill for children and requires much practice. I find this process slower than providing individual maps for each student to copy, but it may help with classroom management.

A classroom teacher could use map copy work as a way for students who finish early to constructively fill in time while waiting on the rest of the class. It would be an easy way to get in an additional subject for quicker students without mandating a designated block of time for geography. In fact, think how much time could be saved if teachers had key memory work from every subject with specific tasks hanging on the walls for students to review when they finish early with class assignments?

What about integrating geography with other course work? I only have so much time available to cover my academic priorities with my students. With elementary age students, I'm more concerned with mastering the basics than with integrating across the curriculum. But anytime a teachable moment arrives, I take it. So, if we are reading about a new place in literature, I have the students quickly sketch where it is. If it comes up on TV, I may pull out the globe and make sure we have located the place. If it comes up on a DVD, we may pause and pull out an encyclopedia. And in a classroom, I would certainly add some geography words to my spelling bees.

I began this chapter with parents at home in mind, and I am ending it with teachers in a classroom setting. But I wish adults who have any contact with children would set aside a few hours and get the world map into their heads. Adults can learn very quickly because they have context. We've watched the news, driven, flown, and traveled. We can relate to the largeness of the globe. We understand the difference between curved 3-D and flat 2-D space. Spend the time needed to improve your own geography skills so that any time a student has a question about a location, there is an interested adult who has an answer ready. Maybe kids will ask a question about geography when there isn't a computer or a map around to consult. Show them that it is useful to be an adult who walks around with a map in her head. Maybe they'll come to think it is normal for people to be familiar with their own planet!

CHAPTER EIGHT

HISTORY

Those who cannot remember the past are condemned to repeat it.
—George Santayana

It's difficult to evaluate an historian's analysis of world events if you don't know the names of the people and places and dates he's referring to. You can't analyze the causes of historical events if you don't first know who did what, where, and when, just as you can't analyze the causes of any subject until you have a basic grasp of its terms and the main ideas associated with it.

In earlier chapters I mentioned memorizing a time line of history. Many schools have bees and prizes in which students memorize a time line of the presidents or a list of the British monarchs or the capitals of states. These events are great for showing students the power of their mental abilities, but if the items memorized are not reviewed repeatedly over many years, they will be forgotten. Classical educators want children to memorize a lengthy world history time line over an extended period of time that stays with them forever.

Classical Conversations' students study the grammar of history in four ways:

1. Memorize a 204-point time line of world events and U.S. presidents in kindergarten through sixth grade.
2. Memorize six short stories of twelve sentences each that summarize a major era.
3. Read lots of stories relating to the memorized time line and the short stories in #2.
4. Copy and rewrite paragraphs from histories.

MEMORIZING A TIME LINE

This is hard rote work for the parent, but your children can do it. When a student actually recites 204 facts for the first time, he will know he can memorize anything. This kind of academic feat excites children with the real joy of doing something well and is a credit to their innate intelligence. Fortunately, children like to memorize, and if you read to them often, they will see quickly the benefit of reciting all those people, places, and dates on a daily basis as they meet them in their reading (as in step #3).

By memorizing a handful of facts each week from our time line, it takes about 25 weeks to go through the entire list. The first 160 facts are memorized 8 at a time, with a week for each set. Eight facts a week over 20 weeks equals 160 facts. Facts 161 and on are a list of the presidents of the United States. We sing the presidents' names in a song, and it only takes a few weeks at most to learn the song. Then we just keep reviewing the song throughout the rest of their education.

The easiest way I know to memorize this many unconnected events is to write eight facts on a board and say them in order. Then erase one fact and say all eight again. Keep doing that until all eight facts are erased and being said by each child without a visual aid. You can do the same activity with a time line of flash cards. Work on the same eight facts all week, and then each day spend a few minutes reviewing facts from previous weeks. Eventually you will have so many facts memorized that you will only want to work on the eight new facts and review a small section of previously memorized facts. I wish I could make it sound more complicated, but all you really do is say the same thing over and over again. I tell the boys to recite their time lines to the dog if there is no one else to listen to them.

MEMORIZING A SHORT HISTORY STORY

Find twelve ideas that are tied to a single era. For example, write a sentence with your child about Christopher Columbus and add ten more fairly chronological sentences about the United States, ending with a twelfth sentence about the War on Terror, and you have your story. I used a child's history book that is out of print to make up the sentences our family memorizes. You can find history sentences from any source you like, but Classical Conversations makes our history sentences available at www.classicalconversations.com as an online service.

As your child memorizes each sentence, have her proceed to the next sentence with a simple conjunction or short phrase that ties the sentences together. "In 1492, Columbus sailed in search of the Indies but instead found a new continent, *and later* the Pilgrims came to New England on the Mayflower in 1620." We have chosen much longer sentences that fill in important facts describing the Mayflower and Columbus, but to start with the sentences can be short as in the example above.

We memorize two stories about the ancient world, two stories about the Middle Ages, and one longer story about America (the equivalent of two twelve-sentence stories). The stories give students a way to connect details of history to their much longer world time line. The goal is to be able to look at your child and say, "Tell Grandma the story of America," and she can! Eventually she'll be able to tell Grandma not only the story, but also the presidents' names in order, and the story of major civilizations that came before and fostered the journey to America.

Often parents want to know what else to do for history in grammar school. It just doesn't seem like enough to memorize facts. Or, on the contrary, it seems too hard to stick with so many facts over an extended period of time. Well, here's my purpose for memorizing the grammar of major historical events: whenever my students learn a new fact they are able to say things like, "That happened after the Civil War," or "The King Arthur stories remind me of Charlemagne and Pepin the Short." Students need a solid context for the rest of their lifelong studies. The splendid narratives of history become more meaningful when one can identify both where and when they took place.

Maybe this is a simpler way to make the point: Can you as an adult tell me in chronological order over two hundred historical facts and summarize major eras in world history? This seems like an obvious goal of history studies. Classical educators know that our children can both know and enjoy history. I would argue that the more history you actually know, the more history you are able to enjoy.

MEMORIZING HISTORY PASSAGES

Young children were taught nursery rhymes as a way to build their vocabulary, instill moral values, and teach beginning reading skills. They easily memorize dozens of silly songs, rhymes, and patriotic melodies. Classical educators take this a step further and encourage students to memorize significant historical articles like the Pledge of Allegiance, the Bill of Rights, the introduction to the U.S. Constitution and the preamble of the Declaration of Independence. Memorize these important documents with your children by reviewing them while waiting at the dentist's office or for a sibling's soccer practice to end.

Unfortunately, most adults today did not memorize nursery rhymes during childhood, let alone significant historical passages. So let's remedy that by memorizing passages of histories with our children. Two generations can work together by memorizing things that tickle our hearts like nursery rhymes, frighten us like *Beowulf*, and inspire our civic spirit like the Gettysburg Address. The phrase "four score and seven years ago" helps me to remember that the American Revolution was eighty-seven years before the Civil War, when Lincoln penned these famous words. Even math creeps into classical conversations!

Classically minded parents quote significant authors like Aristotle, Austen, C. S. Lewis, and Lewis Carroll so often that their children begin to think they are relatives who live in other states. Cicero and Caesar are more than "dead white men" in classical households—their words warn us of the loss of treasured values if we forget the past.

Often an artificial tension is presented between the goal of teaching the basic skills and core content. To classical educators, both are needed. While we emphasize the practice of skills, we need excellent material to practice on. Classical educators go out of their way to ensure that the content is of enduring quality. At first, mastering the classical core could seem like torture if we were not taught to value academic rigor. Eventually, studying history through scholastic literature becomes second nature and begins to be enjoyable.

My high school–age son was recently concerned about an extensive memorization project in Latin. We reviewed the memorization process, the facts that need reciting, and the completion date. He ended the conversation with a sigh of relief, "Oh, is that all?!" He still remembers how hard he has worked, so he approaches new things with some trepidation, but he's been practicing the skills for so long that once he grasps the goal, the large content doesn't stand in his way. With additional maturity, he will develop confidence in both his skills and content mastery.

STORIES ABOUT HISTORY

It's not important to limit yourself to a planned, chronological list of historical world literature. Just read what your family wants to read. The memorized history time line helps us tie stories to their proper order in history. Reciprocally, reading and discussing literature helps to keep the time line fresh in the mind. We do analyze enticing stories about history, but not at the expense of memorizing the time line. Once my students are abstract thinkers, we purposely dig into analyzing history.

One could make the argument that children can begin to really enjoy more in-depth history studies at an earlier age, and I would agree. As you'll see in the following discussion, we do dig deeper. The concern that I have with grammar school today is that we spend so much time trying to get our children to analyze history that our children arrive in high school without having mastered the basics. They had fun exploring history and literature and science, but they don't really *know* any history or literature or science. The basics take so much diligent practice that in our household the "fun" part of studies is experienced more serendipitously, and not as a result of planning to have fun. I am a busy mom. I can only schedule so much time of intense study. The time I schedule has to be purposeful and rigorous. I have to model a love of academics if I want my children to love academics.

When my children were younger and soccer and fencing lessons were finished for the school year, the boys would build models or play with Legos and listen to a CD of Susan Wise Bauer's *The Story of the World*. When it was too hot to go outside, we'd listen to additional books on tape. Now that they are older, we still listen to audiobooks in the car on long trips or in the evening when we draw maps together. We particularly enjoy Bauer's *Story of the World* audios because they are just good stories. While the stories are presented chronologically and in increasingly difficult reading levels, we listen to them in any order. The boys just pull out a disc and we listen. Though the stories come in book form and even include teacher's manuals with activities, we choose to just enjoy the audio version and spend our time reading other material. I read enough to my children and appreciate the opportunity for an adult to read to me.

One story we enjoyed listening to was a story about the Greek mythological hero Odysseus. We've read Homer in many versions, and *The Story of the World*'s version prompted conversations about other versions we had read. When we were listening to the mystery of the citadels along the Indus River (a story about ancient India), we commented on how we could ask our friend from India to tell us more when he came to visit. When the reader pronounced "Mycenaean," she said it with a different accent than we do. I was wondering who's right. Does ancient Mycenaean follow the same pronunciation as modern Greeks? Do we really know how to pronounce the word at all? When we looked up the pronunciation of "Amenhotep," another unusual name, we found four different pronunciations, because no one knows which of the four syllables to stress.

The boys were helping each other with a model helicopter as *The Story of the World* discussed virtue among the Greeks, and I used the moment to point out that they were demonstrating the same virtues of kindness that the Greeks were concerned with. When they fight, I can refer to Achilles and Agamemnon. Then, as the story of Cyrus's birth was told, we discussed how similar Cyrus's infancy was to the story of Snow White.

These seemingly random inquiries or attempts at discussion were all prompted by listening to stories. Seek to initiate and to capture teachable moments. A teachable moment means that we drop whatever we are doing and search for the answer to a question, or try to understand what we can learn from something that has just happened, because children with a question pay much better attention in the moment. One of the main benefits of home-centered education is the ability to answer each student's questions and encourage curiosity because there are so few in the room competing for attention.

My family doesn't study history with textbooks, unless that is what the students choose to read. In high school, we read articles from leadership and political institutions, rewrite American documents in our own words, analyze great speeches, and pore over economics books. We watch Martin Luther King Jr. give his "I Have a Dream" speech in front of the Lincoln Memorial on YouTube and learn about the sacrifice of Leonidas, king of Sparta, on the Discovery Channel. We attend the opera to hear Verdi's "La Traviata," rewrite the sermons of famous Puritans such as Increase and Cotton Mather, and debate international trade policies while practicing our dialectic and rhetorical skills. The abstract understanding will come if the grammar skills are in place.

I used *Story of the World* as an example for integrating stories into real life timetables, but, of course, there are many other interesting books on history. Read the Newbery Medal winners, Dover Classics, and even abridged cartoon versions of history. We really enjoyed the historical graphic novels of Hergé in his famous *Tintin* series. And even in high school, we enjoyed *Adventures in Odyssey* from Focus on the Family. You never know where you'll end up once you enter Odyssey's Imagination Station. As corny as that sounds, they are really good stories that make history come alive.

Parents live with too much guilt. We want it all for our children, yet we often miss the best. I know that my boys have memorized almost three hundred historical events and hundreds of geographical locations. How do I know? Because they can just rattle them off. This is one place where I feel confident that they received the best education they could as young children with very busy parents.

WRITING ABOUT HISTORY

Once you have the habit of memorizing time lines and reading about history, it is time to develop the habit of writing about history. Habits are things done regularly. Memorizing, reading, and writing about history are the habits of a student of history. As I explained in Chapter Five, on writing, classical educators are more concerned that young students learn to imitate good history writers by copying their works than they are about young students writing original, creative literature. There will be time for originality.

In the following passage from *The Autobiography of Benjamin Franklin*, the Founding Father describes how he learned to write:

> About this time I met with an odd volume of the *Spectator*. It was the
> third. I had never before seen any of them. I bought it, read it over
> and over and was much delighted with it. I thought the writing ex-

cellent and wished if possible to imitate it. With that view, I took some of the papers, and making short hints of the sentiment in each sentence, laid them by a few days, and then without looking at the book, tried to complete the papers again, by expressing each hinted sentiment at length and as fully as it had been expressed before, in any suitable words, that should come to hand. Then I compared my *Spectator* with the original, discovered some of my faults and corrected them.

I also sometimes jumbled my collections of hints into confusion and after some weeks, endeavored to reduce them into the best order, before I began to form the full sentences and complete the paper. This was to teach me method in the arrangement of thoughts. By comparing my work afterwards with the original, I discovered many faults and amended them; but I sometimes had the pleasure of fancying that in certain particulars of small import I had been lucky enough to improve the method or the language and this encouraged me to think I might possibly in time come to be a tolerable English writer of which I was extremely ambitious.

This same method is described by Jean Lee Latham in her biography of the early American mathematician Nathaniel Bowditch, and the art of imitating writing is often referred to in children's literature about schools before the 1950s. Dorothy Sayers, in her famous essay *The Lost Tools of Learning* (mentioned in previous chapters), described the art of writing this way:

In certain of the arts and crafts we require a child to "express himself" in paint before we teach him how to handle the colors and the brush. There is a school of thought which believes this to be the right way to set about the job. But observe—it is not the way in which a trained craftsman will go about to teach himself a new medium. He, having learned by experience the best way to economize labour and take the thing by the right end, will start off by doodling about on an odd piece of material, in order to "give himself the feel of the tool."

Before we ask our students to tackle a history report or analytical essay, we need to give them plenty of time to mess around with the tools of writing. Therefore, classical educators spend much time working with our students on the mechanics of writing and copying the writing of great historians. After practicing the tools of writing, we teach students to make note of key words from short history passages. Then, as Mr. Franklin explained, the student retells the same passage in his own words using the key words to spark his memory of the author's message. While discussing the students' rewrites of famous passages, classical educators take the opportunity to teach children the art of writing paragraphs. Students copy sentences to learn mechanics and they copy paragraphs to learn the art of imitating great ideas on paper. During the final proof of the paragraph, return the student's attention to correcting the spelling, punctuation, and grammatical errors of each sentence.

The rewriting of paragraphs on history will not only teach the student to arrange his thoughts in an orderly manner, as Franklin proposed, but he will learn some history at the same time. A memorized time line will enable the student to learn even more history while imitating great authors. So the classical educator concentrates on instructing children in the arts of memorizing, reading, and copying history until children are old enough to rewrite passages from memory about history. Intentionally practicing these basic skills will allow your students to develop a core of history knowledge that they can call upon as adults. As the students mature, they will be able to competently apply history to broader contexts and articulately express their analysis of history's relevance in their own lives.

STUDENTS PRESENTING HISTORY LESSONS

Classically trained grammar students develop a competency in history by:

1. playing games and contests that facilitate memorizing time
    lines and history stories,
2. reading and listening to many stories,
3. copying the best of historical narratives, and
4. practicing their presentation skills by relating history to
    others (as by telling Grandma the story of America, men-
    tioned earlier).

In grammar school, writing essays and presenting them to a class is
not the most important thing to do. However, once the time line is well in
hand, and lots of reading and copying have been practiced, the older
grammar school student should be assigned a weekly paper to present to
his family or to the students he joins to practice memory work. Before you
worry about one more thing being added to your plate, however, let me
show how this can happen naturally.

In kindergarten through second grade, just let the child present an
old-fashioned show-and-tell in which she explains how Daddy gave her
her best pet for Christmas or shares her delight in a new doll.

In third and fourth grades, let the students present a short passage
from historical literature that they enjoyed.

In fifth to sixth grades, occasionally assign five sentences that require
the student to rewrite a history passage of your choosing. But also allow
your children the freedom to present original paragraphs that they have
written about the things they enjoy. If they don't enjoy writing by this age,
let them present their copied or rewritten paragraphs.

Many adults fear public speaking. Classically trained students should
practice presenting material on a regular basis so that they grow up less
fearful of intelligently expressing their ideas to a crowd. Presentations are
not about the material presented, they are about building the child's confidence and poise. Throughout grammar school, just aim for a three-minute
presentation. The hard part should be getting your children *off* the platform, not onto the platform. By being brief and regular in presentations,

while mastering the core features of the classical model, your students will quickly have more to say than three minutes allows.

A child should stand before her audience, look at the crowd, introduce herself, give her presentation, and then ask if there are any questions. These skills can be practiced while talking about a favorite teddy bear, reading a passage from Wilberforce, or reciting Longfellow's "The Midnight Ride of Paul Revere." And the crowd can be family, church congregation, classical community, or the stuffed animals lined up on the bed.

If you did not begin classically educating your children, have them follow the schedule above, but just move more quickly through the earlier stages. Be sure not to go too quickly through copying or rewriting paragraphs. If Ben Franklin had to practice imitating when he was grown, then it follows that our children will benefit from the practice of imitating, too. Of course, students can use presentation time to share what they know about current events, books, science, and anything else. If students give 20 to 30 three-minute presentations per year for six or seven years, they have plenty of time to cover myriad topics, some assigned and others of personal interest. Presentation skills are also practiced until over-learned. (Stand up straight, smile, keep good eye contact with the audience, etc.)

When our children are in high school, they will need to concentrate on understanding and explaining the great ideas that have been important over the course of human history. Let's make sure they can stand still and confidently look the audience in the eye.

TEACHING HISTORY TO A VARIETY OF AGES

One of the difficult aspects of home-centered education is including all your children in as many subjects as possible. This may seem even more difficult with the classical model because it emphasizes skills over content. Students of all ages can listen to a story about Julius Caesar, but some students are too young to write an essay on Caesar. Even parents with the best of juggling skills can get easily overwhelmed.

One of the ways I have dealt with the contemporary educational paradigm that expects 6 textbooks × 4 boys = 24 subjects for Mom to study (yikes!) was to remember that there are only three skills to work on: grammar, dialectic, and rhetoric. While the children are young, I have to purposely work on grammar skills, but dialectic and rhetorical skills can be more enjoyable for all involved. So I worked hard to relearn the basics described in these chapters, gave up feeling guilty that we might be overlooking something, and then I could rejoice at our serendipitous discussions that required higher-level thinking skills. Now that all four boys have moved into the dialectical and rhetorical stage in high school, the two who were classically educated from birth are far more advanced than my first two "guinea pigs" were at the same age, and they just don't need me very often.

In other words, we work very hard on memorizing rules and facts and concrete ideas while practicing reading and writing and arithmetic. Brain training is paramount. Classical educators also spend much time on the fine arts so that sports, music, and drawing are included to train the body's fine motor skills. History and science were not subjects we studied in our home-centered grammar school. Instead we read and wrote and calculated ideas concerning history and science. Even the basic skills of reading and writing were simplified to delight in reading and copying famous authors.

My time with my very young children was mostly spent teaching them self-control and obedience so that they would be physically and emotionally able to follow my instruction. This was very hard to do. But by expecting them to do hard things for a very short amount of time while young and then gradually increasing the time and quantity of the activity as they matured, they became more and more capable. By over-practicing the basics, they needed me less and less as they encountered difficult material.

Some parents may disapprove of the idea of training children to obey, as if they were dogs instead of sentient beings with minds of their own. It may be hard to believe, but inculcating obedience and expecting rigorous effort from our boys has actually helped my children to be free of me. As teenagers, they don't need to obey me any longer because they can confidently make choices and succeed without me policing them. Also, their father has always had even higher expectations for our boys, and now that they are young men, they look to him for counsel and guidance. When I was first grappling with the classical model and home-centered education, I read a book called *Hints on Child Training* that initially offended me in its severity toward children. (It was originally published in the 1890s, written by Henry Clay Trumbull, an American clergyman and a pioneer of the Sunday school movement.) I wanted our home to be delightful. I wanted to have great experiences with my children. But as I completed the book, I began to recognize the enormous love the author had for his children, and that the worst thing I could do was abandon my children to themselves.

Here's a simplistic example that shows how the classical model works in any area. Rather than spend my mothering years yelling, "Shut the door!" in frustration, I trained my boys to shut the front door. When a particular door left ajar brought up the ire in me, I called the boys over and made them repeatedly open and shut the door. I said, "We will have door-shutting lessons until you can remember on your own." It only took a few times, over a period of a year, of me standing there with them while they opened and shut the door properly, but it gave us a lifetime of peace and fewer flies inside!

So even though we want to teach our children to enjoy history, if we take the time to teach them the little things that make history studies possible, such as reading and writing well, we will have much more peace in our family. I don't have to fret over college entrance essays or Advanced Placement history exams. I see my boys finding employment opportunities, working on political campaigns, and engaging in community service. All of these activities give us the opportunity to contribute positively to the history of mankind—at least locally—rather than forgetting and repeating its blunders.

CHAPTER NINE

SCIENCE

We perish from want of wonder, not from want of wonders.
— *G. K. Chesterton*

Classical educators help children to identify scientific principles by:

- Fostering curiosity through the development of observation skills
- Defining and classifying terms that describe the universe
- Conducting experiments and demonstrations to study cause and effect
- Presenting the ideas of influential scientists

If observing, defining, experimenting, and presenting are practiced in grammar school, our rhetorical school students will be able to enjoy discussing both abstract theories and practical applications of science. Understanding the classical sciences allows each of us to appreciate the beauty and harmony of the cosmos while equipping us to participate in the investigative process.

LEARNING TO OBSERVE OUR WORLD

The more I delve into the classical model, the more I realize the goal is to teach young students to be keen observers and to know how to utilize all their senses as they discover how the world works.

My family enjoys finding shark teeth on beaches. These teeth are particularly abundant on the Eastern Seaboard and they are easy to find if you know what to look for. We enjoy helping other beachcombers learn to find shark teeth. Once you discover a single tooth, you begin to see more scattered along the beach. It makes you wonder why they weren't obvious before. As with shark teeth, we often walk past the most interesting aspects of nature.

The same is true about constellations and planets. They are above us every night, waiting to be examined and wondered at, but most of us seem unable to identify space objects, or even to notice the sky is there. We have a friend that is very interested in astronomy and calls us whenever anything unusual is in the sky. She tells us whether to look north or south and how high above the horizon and at what time the object will appear. Through her encouragement, we have learned to identify many of the major features of the northern sky, and we have increased our confidence in the study of astronomy. Fortunately, learning to be keen observers of astronomical features requires us to sit outside at night. Campfires, roasted marshmallows, and flashlights are an important part of astronomy class.

Science studies provide the perfect opportunity to teach children to "see." Eventually, we will want them to see injustice, or a need of the larger community, and know that it is in their power to come up with solutions rather than walk past problems the way a child walks past a dirty shirt on the floor. So, while it may seem like idling to lie on your back and identify cloud formations or name the animals hidden in the clouds' shapes, it is actually an effective and pleasurable way to teach the art of observation and to exercise the imagination.

We also need to teach our children to observe with their other senses. Sitting on a log with your eyes closed and identifying the sound of a nearby stream, an owl, and cicadas develops auditory identification skills. A child who can listen to classical music and identify the various instruments develops a more finely attuned ability to hear the different sounds spoken by a foreign accent or the sounds of a bird call. They also learn how to listen to instructors and parents. Learning to listen will allow them to ask one day about the Doppler effect (the stretched sound heard when one car passes another), or why dogs and young children can hear a broader range of sounds than adults. Listening inspires curiosity. It pleases parents when children observe something special among the mundane. We want our children to have curious, observant senses. So, find opportunities to be quiet as a family. You may be surprised at the roar of heartbeats, distant trucks, fans cooling, and airplanes jetting by.

SCIENCE FACTS

Obviously it is impossible to memorize every fact of science, so it is important to choose foundational facts that frame the major discussions within broad scientific categories and memorize these facts over a long period of time. Rather than memorizing a list of facts as we do in history, I changed the format a little by changing each science fact into a question and answer to memorize. Scientists should learn to ask questions, so this seems like an appropriate way to both memorize data and model inquisitiveness. For example, my students memorize: "What are the types of volcanoes? active, intermittent, dormant, extinct." This is similar to the ancient catechisms used in the schools in Alexandria during the first three centuries AD. The term "catechism" is usually associated with religious instruction, but it is actually a classical method of memorization for any subject, in which a preconstructed set of questions and answers are used to teach precision in responses.

Each week, we memorize one science fact and then determine if we want to write a paragraph on the idea or read a book on the topic or download a related movie. We don't spend much time on planned science activities because the students need time to go outside and explore nature on their own. Over the course of three years, we memorize 72 facts (24 a year), then we continue to drill the questions and answers throughout their education.

A fun way to drill the questions and answers is through a game like Jeopardy! We assign points to a question and the student picks the category. For instance, the child may say, "Biology for 200 points," and I'll ask, "What are the five kingdoms of living things?" If he doesn't correctly respond with, "The five kingdoms of living things are animalae, plantae, fungi, protista, and monera," a sibling or his father gets to answer. If the other family members are much older they can play for zero points just to practice. We also play this game when we meet weekly with other families, so we can compete against a variety of players who are memorizing the same responses.

When I give an idea like this, I'm not suggesting that you try to formalize an actual game. Then you would be using your time making the game board rather than playing the game with your family. Just have a family member get scratch paper and keep points while another gives the questions as the players choose from the science memory work. Why should one question be worth more points than another? Just throw out a question, record the score of however many points your child called out, and move to the next one. Let them say, "Astronomy for 10,000 points." Who cares how many points? Just have fun and play while intentionally learning. It's more fun to drill facts during school hours if you know you may win a game later in the day.

Once parents start to see how much their children naturally memorize, they often want to add even more. Please proceed with caution, though. If you add on so much that you can never systematically review it all, you're back to surveying and drilling for short-term memory. Pick key science facts that will stay with your child for a lifetime.

From kindergarten through sixth grade, we memorize 72 facts. They can be memorized from a sheet of paper or flash cards or a placemat or an audiobook CD or a computer game. Use whatever tools you like to use; just keep encouraging your children to recite their science questions. You are free to develop your own list of science facts or purchase a product that has pulled out the facts for you.

We memorize questions and answers from the following categories:

- **Biology**—classifications and characteristics of living things. Though modern classifications are being replaced by DNA classifications, they are still useful for acknowledging the basic characteristics of species. We can easily see and categorize feathers and scales; we can't see DNA structures.
- **Earth Science**—atmosphere, oceans, landforms, and volcanoes. The basic layers and attributes of our planet are readily defined, though still mysterious enough to prompt curiosity and questions.
- **Environmental Science**—biomes, food chains, and pollution. Within earth science is the study of the interactions of things on earth. With our current concern about things "green," it is important to me that my children actually can define "ozone" and other current environmental terms.
- **Astronomy**—space mission, major space bodies. The Apollo missions are long over with, but the advancement in space research continues to rely on their achievements. Key space projects and the amazing galaxies they reveal form the basic vocabulary for our astronomy studies.
- **Physical Science**—states of matter and laws of motion and thermodynamics. Whether it is Newton or Einstein, their definitions of the states of matter and motion provide the foundation for both three-dimensional and quantum mechanics.
- **Chemistry**—the first twenty elements of the periodic table, including name, atomic weight, and atomic number of each chemical element. The elements in the periodic table determine

cooking ingredients, the analysis of star composition, and the controversies of fertility. The periodic table doesn't change often, is fairly short, reveals the order of the universe, and provides the foundational vocabulary for why things do or don't bind together—so why not memorize it?

- **Origins**—Ideas such as catastrophism, gradualism, rapid-decay theory, and the unified theory of physics may not be in your daily vocabulary, but these words heavily influence scientific leaders and the research politicians will fund. I want my children's ears to perk up when they hear this kind of vocabulary on the news.

DELIGHTING IN DEFINING TERMS

Classical educators begin by teaching children to define terms. You may be getting the impression that the best thing parents can do to educate their young children is to spend time with them naming things. That's right! I told you the classical model was simple. Parents just need to define an ever-broadening range of vocabulary as they learn about new subjects with their children. Identifying, describing, and discussing curiosities draw us together.

Notice what naming can do when taking a walk with the family. When a creature crosses your path, you can simply think "bird," or you can observe the identifying features and think "kingfisher" or "egret" or "swallow" as it flits by. Identifying the bird by color, size, and beak structure allows a parent to grab the child's attention with the words, "Look! A female wood duck heading to her nest in that bald cypress..." Similarly, we have all seen stars, but an evening walk comes alive with comments such as, "There appears to be a plane flying parallel to Orion's belt," or, "Doesn't Venus look especially large this evening?" We feel more intimate with the creation we can name. Otherwise, nature is often rendered invisible, and we miss opportunities to appreciate science in our daily lives.

Science is most naturally studied in categories such as those listed above—astronomy, earth science, biology, chemistry, and physics—in which we name and define elements of the natural world. As we define, observe, or experience new scientific ideas, they can be added to the mind like new items in a grocery store. When I hear the word "cypress," my mind goes directly to the regions where it stores science words about trees. If "cypress" is a new term to me, I need to find out more information about it in order to set it among the natural category of "trees that grow near water" in my mind. The brain categorizes everything to facilitate retrieval, so I want to teach my children not just to name natural features but also to easily organize them by categories.

In science, as with other subjects, children learn new information best through immersion. Every parent naturally names and defines scientific terms when teaching babies and toddlers the names of plants and animals. We teach very young children that birds, dogs, and snakes are animals. Eventually, the groups are further differentiated and identified by specific names such as bluebirds, collies, and asps. Students learn to categorize animals by shared characteristics like feathers, fur, and scales. Eventually we tell our children that animals can be divided by their features into broad categories such as birds, mammals, and reptiles. Defining the framework for scientific study is begun very early for children whose parents are interested in observing the world around them.

As children mature, we want to broaden the categories, definitions, and vocabulary, but there are so many wonderful things to study, it can seem overwhelming. Where to begin? Classical educators actively seek to strengthen students' abilities to think about science in an organized manner. As students encounter new ideas, they are encouraged to place the term in a category such as astronomy, earth science, biology, chemistry, or physics. And they are asked to intentionally memorize specific key words that help the student to "fill the science aisle" in their brains.

For astronomy, students may memorize the order of the planets in the solar system, constellations, definitions of stars, types of stars and galaxies, and the laws of planetary motion. For earth science, students may memorize types of cloud formations, ocean features, and land formations. For biology, students continue naming and categorizing plants, animals, and fungi. For chemistry, they memorize the periodic table of elements. For physics, students memorize basic laws that describe how objects move in time and space, such as Newton's laws of motion and the laws of entropy and enthalpy (in thermodynamics).

Most science textbooks for elementary students do cover the topics listed above. Our concern as classical educators is that science terms are presented in thick books with too much information. The goal becomes to read the textbook and take a test on facts filed in short-term memory. Instead, science memory work for grade-school students should be minimal, meaningful, and intended to be purposefully revisited throughout the students' years in school.

You may wonder why an eight-year-old would need to memorize these sophisticated principles when they can't understand their meaning. The classical educator is not interested in application right now, but focuses on preparing the child for later growth in a field of study. These facts do not have to be taught in context of anything in particular. They are taught in the same way one would teach a nursery rhyme . . . for the pleasure of having words roll off our tongue or the pleasure of learning something well. These concepts become useful later when scientific categories are analyzed and applied in more advanced studies. For example, as the older student balances equations of reactions in studies of physical science, chemistry, and physics, it will become very useful to already have the periodic table of elements memorized.

When we started schooling our children, my husband and I didn't know many of the things to which I refer in this book. For more than twenty years we've been striving to improve the education of our children. In the process, we have begun to improve our own education. It has taken us many years of study to get where we are. I hope that by pointing out the books and ideas that were influential to our appreciation of the classical model, I might shorten the journey for your family.

The primary thing I have learned is that science is at your very doorstep. Kick a rock as you step out of your front door and you might startle a bug or an earthworm. You can learn to appreciate outdoor nature studies by keeping classification books handy. Popular resources include Roger Tory Petersen's field guides to birds, various science and nature reference titles published by Usborne, and flash card sets purchased at local grocery stores. Your family can also attend lectures given by local horticulture societies and travelogue presentations. The "big box" department stores also carry place mats that illustrate basic scientific structures like anatomical features, constellations, and the earth's core. Just remember, if you take a walk or visit a new location, bring an identification book along and soon your family will be seeing minerals and flowers and fungi in a whole new way.

I have developed the memory work that I thought was most foundational to science studies for beginners into three products—an online drill, an audio CD for the car, and a print resource for flash cards and map studies. These products include the science facts that Classical Conversations students review every week throughout grammar school and are now using in their dialectic studies in high school. They are organized two different ways: by weekly memory work and by cumulative subject review. The weekly memory work has the science facts, history sentences, math tables, English grammar, Latin endings, and geography locations on a single sound track so the students can listen to the new memory work for a specific week. The cumulative reviews have an entire subject on one track. If you want to review just the science questions and answers for the year, your child can listen to the science track. Visit ClassicalConverationsBooks.com for details.

By developing a working vocabulary for the basic framework of nature, the whole world becomes material for family conversations. So don't stop the good work of naming and identifying that you began with your toddlers. As you expand your science vocabulary, share it with your children. If you cook or garden or work on cars or build electronics projects, you know a lot of science already. If you develop an interest in nature, you can confidently become a very capable science teacher.

SCIENCE EXPERIMENTS

For foundational academics, don't worry about elementary science experiments lining up with the students' science memory work or the science literature they read. The other things we have to teach, the core skills of reading, writing, and arithmetic need our purposeful attention so that our children are free to research and explore their world. Most memorable science investigations with children are going to occur serendipitously and may seem unrelated to their formal studies. If your children find an abandoned baby bird in the front yard, you are going to enjoy the discovery (and probably try to comfort the little thing), not say, "Leave it to die; we aren't studying birds until next semester." Even an experiment or investigation that is planned and related to schoolwork brings out unexpected, unconnected questions from children's minds. If I had to organize every science fact into a demonstration, I would quickly become weary and be glad for someone else to teach my children. And my children would come to think of exploration as something (rather tedious) that is done to them rather than an adventure to be enjoyed.

Organizing studies around units is efficient for adults who must prepare and lead a class on a single topic for a brief period of time, but unit studies are ineffective for young students trying to master a new topic. Think about it...

Student A is studying plant cells. One week she reads a magazine article on plant cells, and a few weeks later she does an experiment about plant cells. Throughout the year, she works on memorizing the plant cell structure for an end-of-year science bee by sketching its key components. Throughout the semester she gives three-minute presentations on plants and plant features, and she catches an occasional TV documentary on plants.

Student B has a teacher who is going to do a weeklong unit on plant cells. On Monday she introduces the vocabulary of cell structures for a spelling bee on Friday. On Tuesday the class reads about plant cells. On Wednesday the class watches a video on plant cells. On Thursday, they do an experiment on plant cells. On Friday they take a quiz on plant cells and participate in the spelling bee. After a great, intensive week on plant cells, they have to wait another year to have a unit on plant cells.

Which student do you think has the better chance of remembering the structure of a plant cell a few months later? What if the basics of plant cell structure were part of a memorization program that lasted even longer . . . say, from kindergarten through sixth grade? Who do you think will do better in high school biology?

When classical educators intentionally choose science projects, their goal is to reinforce memory work introduced earlier or dialectic skills that will be practiced later. Students focus on core scientific ideas throughout the year and throughout the K–12 experience rather than survey large quantities each year through textbooks.

In kindergarten through sixth grade, my family participates in a weekly science experiment or demonstration that includes a discussion around these questions:

What is the purpose of this experiment?
What are the procedures to complete the experiment?
What are the materials needed for this experiment?
What did you learn from this experiment?

The experiment or demonstration offered may be inexpensive "kitchen science" or a very practical study on a fundamental scientific concept, but we teach good science skills by asking questions and teaching our students to ask questions. Your questions may take a different form than those above, but ask many similar questions. In our family, we participate in a lab once a week throughout grammar school in order to provide an opportunity to ask these questions repeatedly. The asking and answering of questions is more important than the quality of the experiment. Sir Francis Bacon, the father of the scientific method, followed in the pedagogical footsteps of Socrates by formalizing a series of similar questions for all scientists to answer when evaluating cause and effect in the natural world. Classical educators use science experiments for young children to practice evaluating procedures and cause and effect, to explain the use of various materials, and to discuss methods of reducing experimental errors.

By participating in a weekly experiment, students are given the opportunity to use the science vocabulary they are memorizing. Classical Conversations uses *201 Awesome, Magical, Bizarre, and Incredible Experiments* by Janice VanCleave, not because the book contains the best experiments anyone could ever have thought of, but because every experiment or demonstration is structured to facilitate the asking of questions. The experiments are actually excellent and the book provides plenty of inexpensive labs with household products while covering a wide range of science topics. And the experiments are all in one book that can be used for many years with many children, so it is very inexpensive. The directions are easy to follow and can make any parent confident that Mom or Dad can lead a science lab.

RESEARCH AND PRESENTATIONS

One task that a classically educated student practices is developing his or her own textbooks. Students need to know how to make their own vocabulary lists in any subject or language they study and arrange them alphabetically in the notebook they use to record information on that subject. That means we must teach our students to *really study* material and not just answer the questions at the end of a chapter or on a worksheet. They should appreciate glossaries, thesauri, indexes, and dictionaries as tools that help them learn many new things. It is slow for children to look up information compared to just telling them the answer, but saying "Look it up . . ." will make them pay attention so they don't have to look it up again and will give them practice at using references for information. (There are also some fun, serendipitous discoveries of interesting words or facts as they turn the pages toward the item they were looking for.)

Though I'm frequently asked about my favorite historical novels, few parents ask me which science books we read. Science is just not on Americans' minds, unless you cook or are trying to lose weight. The multitude of great science books are so often overlooked that they are abundant on clearance racks at book stores. Go buy a few!

Read science books as frequently as you read novels or historical fiction. I especially like books that combine science with the history of the development of a scientific idea. For the very young, dinosaur and animal books seem to provide the most interest. Some fun novels that combine math and science with stories about young people are *The Phantom Tollbooth*, *Carry On, Mr. Bowditch*, and the Ralph Moody series. Science stories and illustrated texts are suggested in the resource list for this chapter. Be sure to ask friends and librarians about good science books and stories. The Internet has dozens of lists of books about scientists, the history of science, and science facts by topic and reading level. If you start a book and don't like it, put it down and choose another. Science magazines are usually the best source for current information and can be of interest to all ages. We especially enjoyed an article about a diving suit for people who want to jump out of spaceships. (I guess airplanes just don't go high enough for some people!) Scientists develop products every day that never make it into textbooks. So read short articles that can be just as interesting.

Besides the encyclopedia and Wikipedia, we also keep old science texts around the house for reference. Recently, my eleven-year-old son came to me and said he needed a biology textbook to help him with his weekly research paper. We went to the basement and looked through three old texts until we found one at the right reading level. Notice that he was not using the textbook for a daily guide to his science studies. He was using it as an additional reference, like an expanded encyclopedia, for his science research papers.

When researching a topic, I steer my students to texts below their reading level. This way they can concentrate on research and writing skills rather than reading skills. When they are young children, they are only expected to write and present a good science paragraph each week. On the other hand, if they are only going to read about a subject and orally report back to me, a book at or slightly above grade level is preferable.

We assign a weekly topic for the students to write about. Remember, the topic doesn't have to exactly match their weekly memory work or experiments. The paragraph can be on a current science topic, something that interests the student, or a science documentary or a recent field trip. The most important aspect of the research is that they get to practice their rhetorical skills and share what they learned. We want the information to go into their brain, stew there for a while, and come out in the form of an essay or note cards that are read to the family. Then the family can ask questions and discuss the topic. As students get older, they will appreciate sharing their research with a group of students along with their family.

GOALS FOR SCIENCE STUDIES

Classical educators have different goals for studying science than contemporary educators. Modern schooling defines a science education as a biology credit, a physical science credit, and a chemistry credit earned by reading through textbooks and answering the authors' or editors' questions rather than the students'. Analyzing scientific concepts and communicating their ramifications are neglected just when students are ready to exercise higher-order thinking skills. I want my children to practice the dialectic and rhetorical skills while studying high school science so that they are not too intimidated to read great scientific documents or to logically argue with scientific fads such as weight loss schemes or medical scares drummed up for publicity.

The goals for a classical science education are exemplified by the curriculum at St. John's College in Annapolis, Maryland, one of the few actually classical universities in the United States. The students are expected to read these science treatises and many more: Aristotle's *Parts of Animals* and

Generation of Animals, Lavoisier's *Elements of Chemistry,* Galileo's *Two New Sciences,* Newton's *Principia Mathematica,* Darwin's *Origin of Species,* and various papers written by Einstein.

The texts listed above are typical of those read by colonial American scholars. Even though I have an engineering degree, I would find these books challenging to read. My goal is to *begin* to encourage my children to study science classically, to advance their education beyond mine, and to learn with them. We have begun this process by using books other than textbooks for our science reading and using textbooks as reference sources to supplement science writing assignments.

Most parents want their young children to learn enough science in order to prepare for the three survey courses offered in most U.S. high schools: biology, chemistry, and physical science. (Occasionally schools will expect students to take a theoretical physics course, but most just offer conceptual physics courses, hence physical science.) Classical educators want to prepare their students to study original scientific treatises and theoretical math proposals like the students at St. John's. It is important to note that *all* students at St. John's study the science curriculum, not just those who like science or are preparing to be scientists. Classically trained students receive a liberal education there, which means they are equipped to study anything. Other colleges that still teach the classical model, including the sciences, include New St. Andrews in Idaho and St. Thomas Aquinas in New York, among others.

Our students should leave twelve years of science coursework able to study more than the grammar presented in a typical high school science textbook. Students should already be familiar with basic scientific terms from grammar school so they can spend time in high school expanding their core of definitions while researching, arguing, and recording scientific theories, applications, and ethical ramifications. Discussions concerning scientific inquiry should form the majority of our high school students' science studies. Then the coursework of a classical college would be approachable by a larger number of students.

American children can be taught to think like scientists from an early age, by encouraging them to ask lots of questions and to identify lots of terms. Exploration and investigation should be a normal part of a child's day. Classical educators begin stressing in elementary school the grammatical foundations that will make the apprehension of scientific ideas enjoyable throughout a lifetime of learning.

I also think we should be more than a little concerned that a large number of U.S. college graduates with science degrees are from other countries. I welcome anyone who has the credentials to attend our colleges; I just wish more Americans studied the sciences. It is not surprising that cultures that learn many languages and have access to Western technologies have begun to surpass our university graduates in scientific research. In early American universities, Latin was a core requirement for studying the sciences. Scientists and mathematicians used to read and write in Latin, the universal language of Western science (and other learning as well). As I understand more about restoring the classical emphasis on the grammar of language for all fields of study, it has become obvious that foreign language studies develop exceptional scientists. Modern universities have, of course, separated language studies from science studies and have even separated math studies from some science studies. Classical educators are working to recover from this divorce, to repair the breaches.

SCIENCE IN REAL LIFE

Our lives today are removed from basic science. If we had to grow our own crops by understanding weather patterns and horticulture, raise our own food by understanding biomes and animal instincts, butcher our meat by knowing anatomy, and preserve winter supplies by understanding chemistry, we would not need to have very much science education in grammar schools. Today's children don't receive as thorough an understanding of science compared to the child who rose at 4:00 A.M. and helped his mother milk the cows and his father plow the fields. Learning to think sci-

entifically takes an effort by all of us. Since most students no longer participate in preparing their own food from seed to table, science has become a
sort of artificial curriculum brought into a classroom with a textbook to
make it easier for teachers to issue science credits. Science labs seem to emphasize sterility, notebooks, and safety over practicality, efficiency, discovery, and understanding.

So, as parents who love math and science and value rigorous training
of the mind, we have to evaluate how we are going to experience science
with our children. Will we re-create artificial experiments and labs? Will
we use textbooks and make lab notebooks? Will science studies be rele-
gated to an indoor lab? Will we replace computer simulations for animal
dissections? Will we value safety over discovery? How will we model wondering at creation? Will we go on field trips? Will we do all of the above?

Our students will model our attitude toward experiencing science.
Gardening, hunting and fishing, remodeling our home, plucking out
melodies on instruments, and launching bikes from ramps into the lake
are some of the many ways we experience the wonders of science, as well as
more "schoolish" activities such as labs from science texts, taking field trips
to science museums, and watching documentaries.

My family is fortunate to live on a lake with lots of woods around.
Regular pastimes include fishing, birding, and observing foxes and opos-
sums as they steal the cat's food. Even when we had a suburban yard, we
still took walks on golf courses and through parks. No matter where you
live, it is possible to observe and classify the wonders of nature.

A recent week has been a good example of integrating science into our
family life. A store owner gave us some tomato plants he was going to
throw away, and I bought some plants for a party we were having. The boys
planted and watered the garden with me, inspiring my youngest son to ask
for permission to weed! Besides gardening, we are building a new deck, so
the boys measured and dug holes for footers, and measured the diagonals of
rectangles to be sure the footers were squared properly. They used the tape
measure and level while their father wrote down measurements.

While four-wheeling through some woods on an all-terrain vehicle, they shot a rabbit. Their friend's father taught them how to skin it and cook it. Later in the week, we were swimming with a group of friends by a dock when one boy wanted to fish. Just as a father was commenting that the boy would never catch anything with all those folks swimming by the dock, the young man pulled in a four-pound bass, and made us all cheer on the angler while laughing at the elder's assumption that was proved wrong.

Later, Ranger, our friendly dog, jumped into the lake, intending to swim across to greet some people on the other bank. I was in the kayak, so I started to chase after him. William ran along the bank to see if he could help me, while David was swimming to the dam and back. I caught up with Ranger, grabbed his collar, and hoisted him onto my kayak. As I turned around, I saw our lake's heron standing on the shore trying to swallow a bass too large for his throat. As I drew the boys' attention to the heron's struggle on the shore, the dog also saw the bird and became very eager to help the two-foot-tall aviator play with his fish. Meanwhile, William watched the pattern of the current so he could meet me as I drifted to shore. I couldn't paddle and hold the excited dog at the same time. David treaded water while we waited to see what would happen to the large fish gasping in the undersize heron's bill.

The fish finally died, uneaten. The heron seemed to know it had wasted a valuable resource because it coyly ate a few greens and looked around to see if anyone else saw the dead fish floating away. Then the bird flew off (without apologizing for his greedy behavior).

Another day, David and I visited some older neighbors who are avid gardeners. They took the time to give us lemonade and cookies while we walked around the yard naming and smelling and touching perennials. A rose may be as sweet by any other name, but if you want to buy one to plant in your own garden, it helps to tell the horticulturist which one you would like. That night, we slept outside since there was an almost full moon. At one point my son woke from a full sleep and mumbled to me,

"Look Mom, the North Star," and then returned to sleep. I smiled as I looked to the north and saw the bright star and to the south and saw the moon was still staring down on us. Before we went to sleep that night, we had read about the Aurora Borealis. Too bad we live too far south to see it.

Besides the outdoor activities that week, my boys worked on their daily math assignments, watched some science shows on TV, and reviewed the science grammar that they had memorized. William was trying to figure out how to play a tune he could hear in his head and was experimenting with piano keys. All of this happened during the summer, when we are "light" on school and "high" on activities.

Now, how do you bring dogs, herons, fish, currents, kayaks, gardeners, backyards, perennials, and children into the school lab? This is one of the many reasons why we make home the base for our children's education. We can go into buildings and create labs anytime, but science is the study of *real* objects and there needs to be time to *really* experience nature. You may not live on a lake, but I promise you that if you dig a hole under a brick or log, you can experience real science with much smaller creatures. Mice, bats, and snakes have entered our suburban homes, offering opportunities for unusual science studies. We have also raised rats to be fed to rehabilitating raptors, and, of course, we have a cat and a dog.

Some parents will comment that they don't know how to skin rabbits, build decks, or identify the North Star. Well, neither did our family at first. Thanks to the classical model, we're not afraid to tackle new ideas and projects. We study lots of books, look up instructions on how to do just about anything on the Internet, and, most important, we are willing to fail. So what if a footer is poured wrong? Just pour another. The boys were first encouraged to skin the rabbit on their own. When they became frustrated, an adult stepped in and demonstrated what to do. If you don't hunt, it's possible to order animals prepared for dissection from science suppliers. Or buy a whole chicken from the grocer and dissect it. But don't say, "Oh, gross!" then wonder why your family doesn't enjoy science. Exploring science can be wet and messy.

So maybe our family prefers outdoor science and other families will prefer indoor science. Besides construction and dissecting projects, your family can try experiments that teach real-life skills such as cooking or sewing or building radios. Before there was a TV in every home, people had hobbies. There are many wonderful things that families can do well at home together, projects that require real investigation and discovery, and you can develop scientific competency at the same time. No science lab needed!

Classical educators know both naming and doing are required. We don't want to spend time surveying science texts as much as we prefer memorizing science vocabulary, reading science books, writing science papers, asking questions, and spending time appreciating nature. Text and reference books are very helpful in developing the ability to identify scientific terms. Spending unplanned time outside with our eyes open is enjoyable and it's helpful in developing the ability to observe well. Even as adults, we like to share our new discoveries with friends and loved ones. We need to encourage one another to explore through both books and activities.

I want to teach my students to define the structures of the cosmos, to observe the wonders that surround them, and to develop an appreciation for all realms of scientific inquiry. I want to inspire them to explore the natural world through a variety of activities, some scheduled and academic, some real life and serendipitous, and all of value in developing a curious mind.

CHAPTER TEN

FINE ARTS

"It is amazing to me," said Bingley, "how young ladies can have patience to be so very accomplished, as they all are." ... "Yes, all of them, I think. They all paint tables, cover screens and net purses."

—*Jane Austen,* Pride and Prejudice

The classics and fine arts are still synonymous in the minds of many. Those who create and preserve "high culture" in the arts help those of us who are inundated by "pop culture" remember that there is an alternative to the ordinary fare. It takes effort to enjoy classical culture, whether in literature, music, painting, or other forms of art, but, once understood, once the appetite is whetted, we are forever hungry for more. Some recent changes in the approach to fine arts actually offer much hope for the classical educators in our culture.

The fine arts cover a wide range of activities, and it is still commonly recognized that the mastery of processes and basic tools leads to the production of beautiful creations. If you are particularly accomplished at a craft, it may be easier for you to appreciate the classical model, as you know how much time you have devoted to your passion.

DRAWING

I discussed the benefits of copying and drawing in the geography chapter. Of course, these benefits carry over to the drawing of anything—portraits, architectural plans, engineered parts, and graphic designs. Drawing is an important communication tool, hence its emphasis in the classical model.

I have sent my boys to art instructors, taken art lessons with them, and studied drawing at home with books and videos. I highly recommend Ed Emberley's art books for young children because he breaks down complicated drawings into their fundamental components: circles, dots, curved lines, straight lines, and angles. It is amazing to see the pirate ship, decorated with masts and weapons, and platforms that a six-year-old can recreate if they follow Emberley's instructions. As your children work their way through Emberley's dinosaurs, vehicles, animals, etc., read Mona Brookes's *Drawing with Children*. Her text aptly explains the positive influences of learning to draw and sheds light on the philosophy supporting Emberley's techniques that foster such artistic talent in young children. Without using the words "classical model," both of these successful art teachers promote the core skills that enable anyone to draw anything. And guess what they both emphasize? Copying!

Once again the simplicity of the classical model is revealed. Copying enables us to teach ourselves both the fine arts and the liberal arts. So spend time naming the various shapes and structures that you draw as you copy pictures with your youngest children.

PAINTING AND OTHER VISUAL ARTS

While drawing teaches children to position their paper properly, observe the basic shapes, and patiently sketch even complex designs, paint and other mediums teach us to use color and texture. Our family has not put much effort into painting as a subject, choosing instead to include our children in remodeling and gardening projects. Not every craft needs to be taught as an academic subject, although of course there is a grammar to painting and texture. We own stacks of remodeling books and paint charts and fabric swatches. As we design our living space, we pore over these books for untold hours before actually creating a project. This is how we study the grammar of design.

But there is more to print art than remodeling, so we work on one planned art project a week during the school year. *Discovering Great Artists* by MaryAnn Kohl and Kim Solga presents a variety of projects from famous artists that students can mimic. One week we studied Giotto and made paint out of minerals and egg whites, just as he used to do. When we studied Fra Angelico, we glued aluminum foil to our project's surface since we didn't have any silver leaf around the house.

We also regularly visit museums and traveling art exhibitions. The books and curriculum we use are adorned with classical artwork. When we go to museums, the children are able to recognize not just the masterpieces they study, but can even identify the artist or era of a piece that they have never seen before. A Van Eyck looks like a Van Eyck every time!

CLASSICAL MUSIC

I have enjoyed strengthening my music skills while helping my children as they take tin whistle, piano, and guitar lessons. Every accomplished musician knows that the fundamentals of music include note reading, tempo, tonality, and rhythm. Musicians have their own language, which sounds inherently beautiful. Words like mezzo forte, maestro, and melody are just pleasant to say. (Maybe because most of the terms are Italian?)

Though the title is harsh, *Classical Music for Dummies* is a great place to begin a classical music education. The book comes with a CD and a very helpful tool called Listening Outlines. As you play the CD, you can read the accompanying outline, which describes in detail at the appropriate second exactly what you are hearing. Using the proper vocabulary, the listening outline tells you the type of movement, the names of the instruments playing at the moment they join the movement, and why those instruments were chosen, and it provides hints that seasoned musicians know in order to play that section of music well. The pre-reading includes a short biography of the composer and the story behind the composition. Young students listen to this CD as an adult reads the outlines. We occasionally replace our weekly art projects by substituting a weekly listening session for a few months each year.

It seems appropriate to mention poetry at this point, because poems often form the lyrics for music. Suzanne Rhodes's book *The Roar on the Other Side: A Guide for Student Poets* is easy to read while arousing an interest in phrases with a rhythm. Though meant for high school students, it is the kind of book that younger students can enjoy, a portion at a time, if read with a parent. The simple exercises not only include word games and poetry development, but also provide suggestions for ways to describe the world with more descriptive words. Memorizing nursery rhymes also develops an appreciation for poetry, rhythm, and the use of unusual words.

Since music is best appreciated when shared, home-centered educators sing hymns at church, attend the local opera and the community symphony, and listen to a wide variety of music while driving in the car. Take the time to discuss the lyrics and sing songs together. Lyrics and melodies are meant to persuade, to woo, and to console, so be sure to examine the message of each artist. Enjoying music as a family is a simple way to harmonize beauty, mathematical principles, philosophy, and word study all in a short lesson.

DRAMA

Classical education emphasizes performing dramas, interpretive speech, and orations as a natural way to foster recitation skills. Disney's *High School Musical* revived interest in drama clubs and gives me hope that maybe the pendulum is swinging back toward the classical arts. It is a good thing when children spend extracurricular time learning choreography and harmony. Though the revival has fostered more fluff than classical dramatizations, it is a hopeful beginning. The revival of high school plays provides evidence that if the students are interested, they are quite capable of memorizing long lines within a short time.

Classical educators enjoy assigning plays both ancient and modern for students to read in "radio format." Plays are meant to be read aloud, so even if you don't intend to stage a complete production, be sure to gather a few students from other families and let the children read the play together. Assign parts and let the students read the parts in the character's voice while wearing a hat or scarf or cape appropriate to the scene.

Dramatists Play Service maintains an extensive list of plays for all ages that cost less than $10 a copy. In grammar school, my sons have participated in Shakespeare's *Julius Caesar* and Bunyan's *Pilgrim's Progress*. It is really impressive to see such small actors memorize such big roles. They participated with home school support groups in which parents organized the performance for the public. Families are usually invited to participate in community theater, where roles are often offered for children.

ATHLETICS

A sound mind and a sound body were valued by ancient civilizations, with dance, field events, and gymnastics defining classical athletics for over two thousand years, but there is no reason to leave out any of the modern sports. Ballroom dancing has been restored as a popular art, which I find to be another hopeful sign that the classics may be headed for a revival. Both pairs of our boys took ballroom dancing lessons, as have my husband and I. Though we don't dance often enough to become any good, we sure have fun at parties and on vacation.

Opportunities to play individual and team sports are abundant, and except for football, it is possible to play competitive sports in high school without attending an institution. The American Athletic Union, Junior

Olympics, Classic Soccer, First Tee, and many other sports clubs are looking to develop the very best athletes no matter where they attend school.
Swimming clubs propose to develop athletes who receive college scholarships. A truly great baseball player my sons befriended went to Puerto Rico
to homeschool during high school because they allowed him to play on
their farm team. There are many ways to participate in competitive sports
without going to school.

Sports are not a very pressing issue for grammar-school-age students,
as there are many private and public recreational and competitive opportunities for young children. But it is a concern for many parents as they prepare their children for high school. Football seems to be the last sport to
cling to the old paradigm of requiring attendance at a "brick-and-mortar"
school.

HOME ARTS

Another area of growing interest in the classics is the home arts. Cooking,
flower arranging, sewing, and gardening shows have never been so popular. Women may not be netting purses like the highly cultivated ladies in a
Jane Austen classic, but contemporary "Chicks with Clicks" have made
knitting very popular. We value things done well, and I hope that the current revival in quality, classical fine arts will continue and even seep over
into the classical liberal arts.

If nothing else, I think these positive signs reveal a deep desire for a return of the timeless. Maybe our culture is tired of being told that beauty is
in the eye of the beholder, and then wondering why black clothes have become so popular among younger and younger children. It lifts the spirit to
surround oneself with beautiful color and art and music. Think about the
pleasure your children receive when they share a funny poem or even a
joke that has a nice, intelligent play on words. One of the joys of raising
young children to love words aptly spoken is to witness their delight the
first time they actually understand a joke that relies on a complex idea. We

know our children are maturing when figures of speech are no longer a mystery, but an interesting way to relate an idea. Rhymes, songs, poems, colors, texture, and handiwork are simple ways to bring harmony and peace to a child's mind as parents nurture strength and dexterity in a growing body.

CHAPTER ELEVEN

SCHEDULES AND RESOURCES FOR CLASSICAL EDUCATION

All kinds of parents in all kinds of situations are eager to help their children learn. Since no one shares exactly the same lifestyle, please take these schedules as just suggestions for implementing a classical education in your home. With more than twenty years of home-centered education under my belt and as a leader in education, there is one thing I know for sure: children will mess up any schedule you can devise. So do your best and know that I believe you can be your child's best teacher.

IDEAS FOR SINGLE PARENTS

I am always stunned when I meet a single mom or dad who is making a home-centered education work. When parents have a child in need, they can get awfully creative. Many have a grandparent who helps, or they partner with another single parent who shares the schooling responsibilities. Sometimes single parents are receiving medical disability benefits or military pensions or life insurance that helps financially, but I know it can't be easy.

I met one mother whose husband had died, so she worked the graveyard shift and had a friend sleep at their home while she worked. She slept from 7:00 A.M. until noon while her children worked on the computer, practiced piano, did their chores, and played quietly. From noon onward she enjoyed their company. Lots of single parents find home-based employment such as medical transcription, call center work, or online tutoring. Helping a single parent spend time with her children may be the greatest benefit of the work-from-home model.

Here is another idea if you have to work while supporting your children on your own. You could advertise and find four other single parents and organize a small classical school where each of you facilitates one day a week. Then in the evening when you are home you can do as all parents do anyway and have homework time where you catch up on your children's individual needs. I find my children often do their best work at night. They are already played out and want to spend quiet time with me before drifting off to sleep.

IDEAS FOR WORKING COUPLES

The average wage has really dropped over the last few years, and families who find that both parents must work in order to provide for the basics are often in the same predicament as the single parent. Couples in this situation are probably even more motivated to ensure that their children are well educated because they know all too well how hard it is to earn a living. With two of you, maybe you can juggle different days off or work different shifts and "tag team" on the schooling just as you already do for everything else in your family. That is how my husband and I handle work and school. Or you could coordinate your efforts with another family committed to classical education and include the single parent mentioned above.

We shouldn't feel that we either have to teach every subject every day like homeschoolers, or teach nothing like families with students in "brick-and-mortar" schools. There is a middle ground. What if, one day a week, grandmother schooled the kids, two days a week they had a babysitter who was expected to tutor, and the rest of the time one of you were at home with the kids? None of these ideas are perfect. I'm just trying to spark some ideas that may help.

Maybe you want more control over your child's education. Before compulsory education, families with means hired governesses and tutors. That is still an option. You can even have a few families start a small classical school and share the expense of the tutor's salary. It's not necessary to hire several teachers if you can find an educator who understands the classical model and the advantages of the one-room schoolhouse. The tutor's compensation might also be handled through some type of barter arrangement.

CLASSICAL MODEL AT NIGHT

If the only way life works is to have the children in school full-time, don't give up on the classical model. Meet with your children's teachers and ask them how you can help make their school day better with your children. Learn what their goals are for the school year and their expectations concerning homework. If an elementary-age child has more than an hour of homework, don't add to her burden. Just read books with her for pleasure and start training yourself on the classical model. Then when she is struggling, you can actually help her with homework in a way that will be more beneficial than just helping her find an answer.

If your child seems to have little or no homework, identify her greatest weakness and follow the suggestions in this book for that area. Draw maps at night or memorize history facts, or work on copying paragraphs or drill multiplication facts. But don't do too much. Treat it like a regular homework session, an hour at the most.

One reason why many parents begin homeschooling is that their child has so much homework that the parents feel as though they are already homeschooling each evening. If your child is having to spend more than two hours on homework at night (besides reading novels) and is in elementary school, something is wrong. The child should be able to study the basics in six hours a day at school with some quiet studies added at night.

CLASSICAL MODEL IN NONCLASSICAL SCHOOLS

If you are a teacher at a nonclassical school, you can probably fit in a classical education while meeting the state standards. In fact, if you treat the extra work as a game and tell the students that you will be in trouble if you teach them too much, they may become your greatest allies. Children love to "get in trouble" or "cross the line" when an adult is in charge. It's like being bad with no consequences!

If you are teaching a single subject, open and close the hour with two minutes of memory work related to the subject. Keep it prominently displayed on the wall, and tell your students to memorize it when they are waiting for breaks or for other students to complete tasks. Andrew Pudewa, a great classical educator, makes memory work the price for admission into his classroom. The students line up near the door, and each one has to recite the memory work to get in. The least confident students will line up in back so they can hear the most confident students rattle off the "passwords."

If you can get the other teachers to practice a different subject's memory work for two to four minutes a day, the students will memorize core knowledge from multiple subject areas by the end of the year. The trick is not to change the memory work for the next year. Keep it exactly the same so that when a child has been through your school for many years, you can be confident that she will leave your keeping with a positive memory of a definite contribution you made to her education.

I have a friend whose fourth-grade teacher seemed like the worst teacher of all to her as a child. For one semester, he made them copy the verb conjugations for the entire hour. Now in her fifties, she describes him as the smartest teacher she ever had because he made the students do the hard work while he just watched. He already knew the conjugations. Why should he have to work hard?

I don't think we should teach that way, exactly, but he was surely on to something. What would happen if, for the first two minutes of each hour, your students copied a passage or table of information, then spent two minutes racing to messily reproduce the work on scrap paper? I know they would walk into class excited to sit down and beat the teacher's efforts, because that is what I did for years as a grammar tutor. No one ever complained about the "Beat Mrs. Bortins" game. My students were happy to beat me by writing down irregular verbs or the table of squares or whatever I asked faster than I could write them down. They would beg me to let them determine what the class should memorize next because they thought they could beat everyone else.

Even my slowest students had an equal chance of winning because I would handicap each race, just as they do in golf. In other words, a six-year-old may only have to write down four multiplication equations in two minutes, while the eleven-year-olds had to write twelve and I had to write fifteen. It was a truly proud moment for a student when his handicap changed because he was getting to be too fast and he knew Mrs. Bortins didn't like to lose.

A SCHEDULE FOR CLASSICAL EDUCATION AT HOME

Here is our schedule. It changes as the day or child demands, but in general it has worked for many years. It allows plenty of time for doing laundry, cleaning up flooded bathrooms, calling insurance agents for quotes, gardening, and just hanging around. It only adds up to four hours a day, but remember that the time is very purposeful. Studies show that of the six hours students spend in school, less than one-third is spent on intentional academics. The rest is used up by shuffling from class to class and waiting for everyone to quiet down.

7:00	**Bedroom and Breakfast**—Get up, clean up your room, eat, shower, and take care of the dog.
8:00	**Bible Study**—We read the scriptures as outlined earlier in the book so that we get our most important discussions completed for the day. (We generally study while lying around in our king-size bed.)
8:30	**Saxon Math**—We all sit at the same table and work so I can answer questions as needed.
9:30	**Language Arts**—This is my instructional time at the white-board. While I teach one student, the other is copying or writing. With more than two children, this would be the hardest task for the parent to juggle. Start with everyone at the whiteboard listening to your instruction. Then, as you get deeper into parsing sentences or outlining for paragraph rewrites, let the younger children trickle off to play while the older students remain seated.
11:00	**Draw** maps and review time line cards. While the older students draw and drill, use this time to teach phonics to younger children.
11:30	**Break** for chores, lunch, errands. We drill our science, history sentences, Latin, math, and English memory work while in the car using CDs or flash cards.
Afternoon	for anything we missed, sports, and friends.
8:00 P.M.	Bedtime reading as described in Chapter Four. Some time reading out loud and children fall asleep reading (or listening to an audio story if a pre-reader.)

Success comes from doing schooling every day and not missing opportunities to do more when lying around sick or when it is raining or too hot to be outside. Also, one day a week we join our Classical Conversations community for seven hours and work very intensely on memory work games and art and science projects, along with presenting the papers we wrote at home.

Science and history are not given separate attention. They are integrated into the memory work, into reading in the afternoon and evening, and as we imitate paragraphs.

HOW A CLASSICAL EDUCATION GIVES US SKILLS WE NEED AS ADULTS

General terms such as "homo sapiens," "mankind," and "people" are synonymous with "human race," while terms like "parent," "employee," "citizen," "neighbor," and "friend" describe our relationships. Professional titles such as doctor, lawyer, engineer, teacher, craftsman, and contractor define us even more specifically. As we identify ourselves by increasingly narrower titles, the education and training required to fulfill our role can differ greatly. A glassblower needs a different set of specific skills than does a pharmacist. Or so it seems. But don't both need to know the properties of the elements they combine? Don't both of them have to be able to communicate with customers? Don't they both need to be able to read the directions describing a new process, and shouldn't they both have the integrity to throw away inferior products? Common skills that are required by all people are emphasized in a classical education.

As a parent, I don't know what my children will do with their lives. It's their choice. I do know that I want them to find purpose in work and joy in their daily tasks, not because they are the best at what they do, or because they have the most friends or money or anything else, but because those are qualities that inherently make them human. Whether they become craftsmen or professionals, I hope they are competent and content because of the satisfaction derived from a job well done.

As a classical educator, I know it is impossible to prepare my students for the specifics of their future. I am trying my best to equip them with the skills that will serve the broadest of purposes. As a parent, my role is to see that my children are prepared to be confident and competent *generally*. As they become adults, they will need to take over the responsibility for educating themselves *specifically*. For this to occur, I must help my children to develop a core of common knowledge and critical skills. Rigorous academics provide an opportunity for children to master general competencies so that when they are grown they can continue to learn on their own.

The classical model uses the trivium to teach children the basic skills required to absorb, process, and perform. Even though the content they memorize, comprehend, and utilize will be different depending on their specific talents and careers, the art of learning can be generalized in preparation for any endeavor. Practicing the trivium allows students to master the arts of grammar, dialectic, and rhetoric so they can apply these general skills to specific tasks for the rest of their lives. Adults adapt more easily to changes in employment or unusual opportunities if they are confident they can quickly become competent in new areas of information and relationship. Immersing oneself in new information, or "learning the ropes" can be exciting rather than intimidating.

Not only does a classical education instill in us the *tools* of learning, it also allows us to evaluate both the follies and the wisdom of the past in comparison to the predicaments and challenges of the present so that we will be less likely to make costly mistakes in the future. Individuals can make choices based on

1. what they have personally experienced, or
2. they can include the advice of their contemporaries, or
3. they can weigh the value of centuries of ideas.

The classical tradition calls us to value all three in each of our endeavors. Rather than abandoning us to the moment, the classical model immerses us in the great classical conversations of mankind so that we can hear the voice of experience, discuss our present options within our community, and make choices with confidence that we have really done our best. The classical *tools* allow us to include classical *content* in our decisions.

Our current educational model is changing. The world is smaller and the base of knowledge is broader. The options for additional years and types of education change every week. Some technologies and academic systems provide amazing opportunities. Others are just a way for someone to capitalize on the fears of parents worried that their children are missing something new. I believe parents want their children to become free men and women who can master a situation rather than be inundated by sweeping tides of change or stifled by an inability to adapt. I believe parents want to take a moment to evaluate the purpose of education in order to move forward with conviction and purpose as they choose the type of schooling their children will receive. The classical model asks us not to replace the modes and methods of the past with new technologies just because they are new. The classical model also requires that we adopt new forms of communication in a manner that contributes to the highest goals of civilization. I believe parents can wisely utilize new technologies while preserving the qualities that endow children with the ability to find their purpose in life and contribute to the great classical conversations of mankind.

RESOURCES

INTRODUCTION

Bauer, Susan Wise. *The Well-Educated Mind: A Guide to the Classical Education You Never Had.* New York: W. W. Norton, 2003.

This book offers brief, entertaining histories of five literary genres—fiction, autobiography, history, drama, and poetry—with detailed instructions on how to read each type. The lists at the end of each chapter preview recommended reading and encourage readers to make connections between ancient and contemporary writing.

Bauer, Susan Wise, and Jessie Wise. *The Well-Trained Mind: A Guide to Classical Education at Home.* New York: W. W. Norton, 1999.

This book explains, step by step, how to give your child an academically rigorous, comprehensive education from preschool through high school—one that will train him or her to read, to think, to understand, and to be well-rounded and curious about learning.

Bortins, Leigh. *Echo in Celebration: A Call to Home-Centered Education.* Seven Lakes, NC: Classical Conversations Multi-Media, 2007.

Echo is an easy-to-read book that invites you to consider the classical model and home-centered education.

Mulroy, David. *The War Against Grammar.* Portsmouth, NH: Boynton/Cook, 2003.

Mulroy, a Stanford graduate and classicist, begins by laying out the problems associated with the disappearance of formal grammar training from American schools. He goes on to examine the history of formal grammar training and argues its importance in all fields of study.

Wilson, Douglas. *The Case for Classical Christian Education.* Wheaton, IL: Crossway Books, 2003.

America's schools are flunking the test. Building upon his book *Rediscovering the Lost Tools of Learning,* Wilson says we must turn to Christian classical education, with its emphasis on the ancient division of learning geared to childhood development. Wilson will open your eyes to the reality that education is not the world's savior—education itself needs to be saved.

CHAPTER ONE: WHAT'S WRONG WITH EDUCATION TODAY?

Bauerlein, Mark. *The Dumbest Generation: How the Digital Age Stupefies Young Americans and Jeopardizes Our Future (Or, Don't Trust Anyone Under 30).* New York: Tarcher, 2008.

Bauerlein discusses how online access to education is ignored by students, who use the Internet primarily to become immersed in pop culture.

Lewis, C. S. *The Abolition of Man.* New York: HarperOne, 2001.
———. *The Screwtape Letters.* New York: HarperOne, 2001.
———. *The Chronicles of Narnia.* New York: HarperCollins, 1994.

Lewis's collection of seven children's fantasy novels set in the world of Narnia: *The Magician's Nephew; The Lion, the Witch, and the Wardrobe; The Horse and His Boy; Prince Caspian; The Voyage of the Dawn Treader; The Silver Chair;* and *The Last Battle.*

National Association of Adult Literacy (NAAL). Washington, DC: National Center for Education Statistics. Available online from http://nces.ed.gov/naal.

NAAL is a national assessment of English literacy in English among American adults, sponsored by the U.S. Department of Education.

The National Assessment of Educational Progress (NAEP). Washington, DC: National Center for Education Statistics. Available online from http://nces.ed.gov/nations reportcard.

Part of the U.S. Department of Education, the NAEP measures student progress in various subject areas in the nation's public schools.

Paine, Thomas. *Common Sense.* Pamphlet. Philadelphia: R. Bell, 1776. Available online at http://www.ushistory.org/PAINE/commonsense/singlehtml.htm.

Postman, Neil. Introduction by Andrew Postman. *Amusing Ourselves to Death: Public Discourse in the Age of Show Business.* New York: Penguin, 1985.
———. *The End of Education: Redefining the Value of School.* New York, Vintage Books, 1996.

In both books, Postman, a cultural analyst, describes the results of postliterate education.

Sayers, Dorothy L. *The Lost Tools of Learning.* Lecture. Oxford, UK: Oxford University Press, 1947. Available online at http://www.gbt.org/text/sayers.html.
    This foundational essay lays out the problems with modern educational philosophy and calls for a return to the classical model.

To Read or Not To Read: A Question of National Consequence. Washington, DC: The National Endowment for the Arts, 2007. Available online at http://www.nea.gov/research/ToRead.pdf.

Waugh, Evelyn. "Scott-King's Modern Europe." In *The Complete Stories of Evelyn Waugh,* pp. 328–376. Boston: Little, Brown, 1999.
    This popular writer's defense of the classics and all that is enduring is told through the eyes of a man transported from the thirtieth century to the fictitious "Neutralia."

CHAPTER TWO: WHY WE NEED CLASSICAL EDUCATION

Aristotle. *Rhetoric.* Translated by W. Rhys Roberts. Available online at http://classics.mit.edu/Aristotle/rhetoric.html.
    Though difficult to read without a classical education, this book is foundational to those moving out of the grammar skills into the higher-level thinking skills. It provides the launching point for many modern classics on rhetoric skills.

The Association of Classical & Christian Schools. Moscow, ID. Available online at http://accsedu.org.

Bridges, William. *Jobshift: How to Prosper in a Workplace without Jobs.* Cambridge, MA: Da Capo Press, 1995.
    Interesting studies on the age of global technologies. Though slightly outdated, this book formed the conversation about returning to work at home.

Gamble, Richard M. *The Great Tradition: Classic Readings on What It Means to Be an Educated Human Being.* Wilmington, DE: ISI Books, 2007.
    A great collection of short stories and essays that demonstrate the value of a classical education.

Handy, Charles. *The Age of Unreason.* Foreword by Warren Bennis. Cambridge, MA: Harvard Business Press, 1991.

Handy predicts that the twenty-first century will be the Age of Unreason and focuses on the philosophies undergirding our responses. He includes ideas on business and their relationship to family.

Moody, Ralph. *Mary Emma and Company.* Lincoln: University of Nebraska Press, 1994.
My personal favorite read-aloud is the Ralph Moody series on his life as an occasionally schooled youth who must care for his mother and siblings. If I say more, I'll ruin the stories. Just read them all.

The National Home Education Research Institute. Salem, OR. Available online at http://www.nheri.org.
Brian Ray collects data on education and assesses the progress of children whose parents are actively involved in their education. Since few parents homeschool for a lifetime, he also offers analysis for those who are at least highly involved.

O'Brien, Dominic. *Learn to Remember: Transform Your Memory Skills.* London: Duncan Baird Publishers, 2000.
————. *How to Develop a Brilliant Memory Week by Week: 52 Proven Ways to Enhance Your Memory Skills.* London: Duncan Baird Publishers, 2006.
Both of these books are very easy to read, inspiring, and highly practical.

Wiggin, Kate Douglas. *Rebecca of Sunnybrook Farm.* New York: Puffin, 1995.
Just a fun book that reveals the culture of America in the South.

Wilder, Laura Ingalls. *Little Town on the Prairie.* New York: HarperTrophy, 1971.
The true story of a Midwestern family that lived the classical model.

Wilson, Douglas. *Recovering the Lost Tools of Learning: An Approach to Distinctively Christian Education.* Wheaton, IL: Crossway Books, 1991.
Douglas Wilson, director of the renowned Logos School, introduces a model for distinctly classical, Christian education as a response to the current malaise in public education. This is a book by a parent for parents who want better for their children.

————. *The Case for Classical Christian Education.* Wheaton, IL: Crossway Books, 2003.
America's schools are flunking the test. Building on his book *Recovering the Lost Tools of Learning,* Wilson says we must turn to Christian classical education, with its emphasis on the ancient division of learning geared to childhood development. Wilson will open your eyes to the reality that education is not the world's savior—education itself needs to be saved.

CHAPTER THREE: HOW CLASSICAL
EDUCATION CAN HELP YOU

Cothran, Martin. *Classical Rhetoric with Aristotle: Traditional Principles of Speaking and Writing*. Louisville, KY: Memoria Press, 2003.
> Much easier to read and use than Aristotle's original work. Cothran makes rhetorical skills accessible to any older student or parent.

DeGenova, M. K. "If you had your life to live over again: What would you do differently?" *The International Journal of Aging and Human Development* 34.2 (1992): 135–43.

Dokoupil, Tony. "Why Young Men Delay Adulthood to Stay in 'Guyland'." *Newsweek*. Online edition. August 30, 2008. Available online at http://www.newsweek.com/id/156372.

Kern, Andrew. "Leadership Development: Headmasters." Concord, NC: CiRCE Institute, 2006. Available online at http://www.circeinstitute.org/s_headmasters.shtml.

Kirk, Russell. *Eliot and His Age: T. S. Eliot's Moral Imagination in the Twentieth Century*. Wilmington, DE: ISI Books, 2008.
> In addition to interesting comments on Eliot's poetry, this book provides great insight to the differences between those who want to conserve classical values and those who promote "progressing" beyond the idea that core values even exist.

Madison, James. "Federalist No. 47: The Particular Structure of the New Government and the Distribution of Power Among Its Different Parts." *The New York Packet*. New York, 1788. Available online at http://thomas.loc.gov/home/histdox/fed_47.html.
> Though difficult reading for contemporary Americans, all of the Federalist papers speak to current political events. A great defense for those who enjoy living under the original intent of the U.S. Constitution.

Nance, James B., and Douglas J. Wilson. *Introductory Logic* and *Intermediate Logic*. (Nance is the sole author of *Intermediate Logic*.) Moscow, ID: Canon Press, 2006.
> In these books directed toward junior high students, Douglas Wilson and James Nance train students in the crucial skills of defining terms, recognizing basic types of statements, arguing with syllogisms, arguing in ordinary language, and identifying informal fallacies. These accessible texts provide students with a rigorous course in logic that will help them excel in every other subject they study.

Ross, Ishbel. *Journey into Light: The Story of the Education of the Blind.* New York: Appleton-Century-Crofts, 1951.
  A delightful summary of the life of Helen Keller, a truly great American who overcame her limitations rather than letting them define her.

Shakespeare, William. *Henry V.* Dover Thrift Edition. Mineola, NY: Dover, 2003.
  A fun book to read aloud among a "band of brothers," whether related by blood or a love for the classics. Every boy should learn to love this play.

Zacharias, Ravi. *Jesus Among Other Gods: The Absolute Claims of the Christian Message.* Nashville, TN: W. Publishing, 2002.
  A discussion about the portrayal of Jesus in light of Muslim and Hindu theology. Written by a popular author from India, this book examines the case for absolute versus relative truth and the use of words and semantics to persuade. Ravi is an expert when it comes to relating expressions of popular culture around the world to classical ideas that define the humanities.

CHAPTER FOUR: READING

Adults wanting to improve their own ability to read great literature can start with any of the Newbery Medal–winning books for children.

Adler, Mortimer J., and Charles Van Doren. *How to Read a Book.* New York: Touchstone, 1972.

Anthony, Susan C. *Spelling Plus: 1000 Words Toward Spelling Success.* Anchorage, AK: Instructional Resources, 1999.
  Spelling Plus emphasizes the 1,000 base words that constitute 90 percent of English writing. Personal words keep gifted spellers challenged while giving poor spellers the repetition and practice they need. The book includes worksheets.

Douglass, Frederick. *Narrative of the Life of Frederick Douglass, an American Slave.* Dover Thrift Edition. Mineola, NY: Dover, 1995.
  The description of how a slave taught himself to read, enabling him to eventually purchase his freedom and move toward becoming an influential advocate of freedom for all.

Greenholt, Jennifer. *Words Aptly Spoken* series. Seven Lakes, NC: Classical Conversations Multi-Media, 2005–2008.

Words Aptly Spoken: Short Stories
Words Aptly Spoken: American Documents
Words Aptly Spoken: Children's Literature, parts A, B

Words Aptly Spoken: American Literature
Words Aptly Spoken: British Literature
> These literature study guides include thought and review questions about major works of classic literature in a variety of genres and periods. Each guide also includes exercises for students to practice their writing skills in relation to the literature they are reading.

Sire, James W. *How to Read Slowly.* Wheaton Literary Series. Colorado Springs, CO: Shaw Books, 2000.
> A smaller, easier to read tome than Adler and Van Doren's *How to Read a Book.* Sire explains the many ways to read efficiently and effectively, depending on the type of book and the goals of the reader.

Spalding, Romalda Bishop, and Walter T. *The Writing Road to Reading: The Spalding Method of Phonics for Teaching Speech, Writing and Reading.* New York: HarperResource, 1990.
> The best for those who want to know the nature of reading so they can teach students with any level of ability to read.

CHAPTER FIVE: WRITING

I recommend that every adult, even those who don't teach or have children, work through the following four books. They will provide you with the equivalent of twelve years of English language studies.

Kern, Andrew. *The Lost Tools of Writing.* Concord, NC: CiRCE Institute, 2009.

Pudewa, Andrew. *Teaching Writing: Structure and Style.* Atascadero, CA: Institute for Excellence in Writing, 2001.
> This 9-DVD set includes the full teacher training course on 6 DVDs (twelve hours plus practicum assignments), along with 3 two-hour demonstration lessons showing the first step of the process being taught to students at three different grade levels.

Spalding, Romalda Bishop, and Walter T. *The Writing Road to Reading: The Spalding Method of Phonics for Teaching Speech, Writing and Reading.* New York: HarperResource, 1990.
> This is my favorite book that teaches adults how to teach handwriting, phonics, spelling, and reading to children because it gives a complete overview of the skills that develop competent readers and spellers.

Wilson, Nancy. *Our Mother Tongue: A Guide to English Grammar.* Moscow, ID: Canon Press, 2004.

Nancy Wilson surveys the major concepts in English grammar for beginners at the late elementary and junior high level, and even adults seeking a brushup.

Then purchase for a lifetime of reference while improving your language skills:

Strunk, William, Jr. and E. B. White. *The Elements of Style*. Boston: Allyn and Bacon, 1999.
    A fundamental resource for writers, editors, and students since 1959, the slim volume contains the combined wisdom of Cornell University English professor William Strunk Jr. and legendary *New Yorker* writer E. B. White. Though there are other books on the market that delve more deeply into matters of grammar and style, this is the best single source for anyone who desires a pithy, lively guide to the essentials of effective writing.

Warriner, John E. *English Grammar and Composition: Complete Course*. Orlando, FL: Harcourt Brace Jovanovich, 1988.
    This 1957 text contains everything about sentence structures and classifications in a single text. Excellent.

CHAPTER SIX: MATH

Bortins, Leigh. *Tables, Squares, and Cubes*. Seven Lakes, NC: Classical Conversations Multi-Media.
    This book provides tables and self-teaching methods to help students master the multiplication table and the common squares and cubes seen in algebraic equations. The book is inexpensive, nonconsumable, and multisensory, so parents can help all their children master multiplication basics.

Kressin, Keith I. *Understanding Mathematics: From Counting to Calculus*. San Diego: K Squared Publishing, 1997.
    Kressin's book is an easy-to-read, nontechnical discussion covering a broad range of math topics, with emphasis on real-world examples and practical applications.

Ray, Joseph. *Ray's Arithmetic Series*. Eight-volume set. Fenton, MI: Mott Media, 1985.
    Originally produced and used in the late 1870s and 1880s, *Ray's Arithmetic* teaches math from the ground up, developing the building blocks of knowledge and then progressing to more complicated operations. From the beginning, Ray incorporates word problems to ensure that students understand the application of mathematical concepts.

Reed, Art. *Mastering Algebra "John Saxon's Way."* DVD Teaching Series. Enid, OK: AJ Publishers, 2009.

————. *Using John Saxon's Math Books.* Enid, OK: AJ Publishers, 2009.

Saxon Math. New York: Harcourt Achieve.
> Saxon's incremental process teaches students to master old concepts and enjoy the challenge of new ones. Saxon is a complete K–12 curriculum. No curriculum is ever perfect, but Saxon can take a homeschooled student through Algebra II and even beyond without the guidance of an expert math teacher. Placement tests are available at http://www.saxonpublishers.com.

Saxon Math DVDs. Teaching Tape Technology. Chelsea, AL. Available at http://www.teachingtape.com.
> These DVDs, updated yearly, can be used by anyone to either complete a K–12 math curriculum or to train yourself to teach K–12 math through calculus. The teacher explains every lesson in every Saxon Math text using clear examples, the proper vocabulary, and in an approachable manner.

CHAPTER SEVEN: GEOGRAPHY

NationalGeographic.com and EnchantedLearning.com have lots of great maps and map games. Use their maps to trace until your student is confident enough to copy from a map onto a blank piece of paper.

Classical Conversations Connected Community also has a lot of maps to memorize, along with history facts and stories, multiplication tables, and much more. The public library can be accessed at http://classicalconversations.com/registered/index.php?option=com_content&task=view&id=70&Itemid=198

Compact Atlas of the World. New York: DK Publishing, 2005.
> The *Compact Atlas* has many facts to add to your maps besides political boundaries and physical features. This atlas is a great geography reference book for home and classroom.

CHAPTER EIGHT: HISTORY

Adventures in Odyssey. Radio Show. Colorado Springs, CO: Focus on the Family, 1987–2009.
> Since 1987, Focus on the Family has produced over six hundred episodes in this values-based audio drama series set in Whit's End, a fictional small town in America. Many of the adventures include trips to the past where children meet very exciting patriots and scholars.

Bauer, Susan Wise. *The Story of the World* series. Charles City, VA: Peace Hill Press.
> The Story of the World is an award-winning resource for families told in the straightforward, engaging style that has become Susan Wise Bauer's

trademark. This four-volume set covers human history from ancient times to the present.

The Story of the World, Vol. 1: Ancient Times
The Story of the World, Vol. 2: The Middle Ages
The Story of the World, Vol. 3: Early Modern Times
The Story of the World, Vol. 4: The Modern Age
Franklin, Benjamin. *The Autobiography of Benjamin Franklin.* Mineola, NY: Dover, 1996.

> First published in 1793, Franklin's autobiography vividly depicts life in Philadelphia during the Colonial and Revolutionary periods of American history.

Hergé. *The Adventures of Tintin.* New York: Little, Brown Books for Young Readers, 2008.

> This series of comic strips featuring Belgian reporter Tintin became popular in the 1920s, and was later translated into English from the original French. Tintin's adventures are set against the historical backdrop of the Bolshevik Revolution and World War II.

Zeman, Anne, and Kate Kelly. *Everything You Need to Know About American History.* New York: Scholastic Reference, 2005.

> These guides contain the facts and processes that fourth-, fifth-, and sixth-graders—and their parents—either never knew, don't remember, or need explained another way. Each book contains facts, formulas, and procedures and is presented in a visually stimulating format, using full-color charts, graphs, diagrams, illustrations, photos, timelines, and maps.

CHAPTER NINE: SCIENCE

Comstock, Anna Botsford. *A Handbook of Nature Study.* Ithaca, NY: Comstock Publishing/Cornell University Press, 1986.

> First written in 1911, this comprehensive guide to the study of nature is still widely used. In addition to guides for studying plant and animal life, Comstock's book also discusses the role of nature study in education and the limitations of scientific knowledge.

Distasio, Joan. *Biology: 100 Reproducible Activities.* Grand Rapids, MI: Instructional Fair, 1999.

> Diagrams, puzzles, multiple choice, and matching columns enhance the biology text and laboratory experience. These worksheets cover every area of biology, including cells, plants, laboratory equipment, animals, and insects.

RESOURCES 227

Eldon, Doug C., Dorry Eldon, and Bobby Horton. *Lyrical Life Science, Vol. 3: The Human Body.* Corvallis, OR: Lyrical Learning, 1998.
These books use music and lyrics to teach scientific concepts and help students memorize information by setting it to popular songs.

National Audubon Society. *Field Guides.* New York: Alfred A. Knopf.
————. *Pocket Field Guides.* New York: Alfred A. Knopf.
Audubon produces more than twenty full- and pocket-size identification guides with photos and descriptions of birds, wildflowers, trees, mammals, insects, fish, and more.

Pearcey, Nancy, and Charles Thaxton. *The Soul of Science: Christian Faith and Natural Philosophy.* Wheaton, IL: Crossway Books, 1994.
A look at the differences between the classical view of the world as an organism, the modern view that the world is a machine, and the postmodern view that the world is a work in progress.

Peterson, Roger Tory. *Birds: Peterson's Field Guide Color-in Book.* New York: Houghton Mifflin Harcourt.
The classic field guide presented as a coloring book for children so they may investigate the details that help us to identify different species of birds.

Rogers, Kirsteen. *Usborne Internet-Linked Science Encyclopedia.* London: Usborne, 2009.
This illustrated book is a great general reference for ages 9 to 12. The book includes 1,000 recommended websites for further study, allowing students to learn as much or as little as they want about physics, chemistry, biology, IT (information technology), earth sciences, and astronomy.

VanCleave, Janice. *201 Awesome, Magical, Bizarre and Incredible Experiments.* New York: John Wiley & Sons, 1994.
This book is a treasury of science experiments designed to show children that science is more than a list of facts—it is fun! The book guides kids through the steps necessary to successfully complete an experiment, teaching them the best method of solving problems and discovering answers. 201 short experiments cover five different fields: astronomy, biology, chemistry, earth science, and physics.

CHAPTER TEN: FINE ARTS

Brookes, Mona. *Drawing with Children.* New York: Tarcher, 1996.
This easy-to-follow, lesson-by-lesson approach to drawing is for children of all ages and beginning adults. The book guides readers through the basics

and gives important advice for creating an environment in which creativity can flourish.

Kohl, MaryAnn F., and Kim Solga. *Discovering Great Artists.* Bellingham, WA: Bright Ring Publishing, 1997.
This book contains 110 fun and unique art activities for children to experience the styles and techniques of the great masters, from the Renaissance to the present. A brief biography of each artist is included with a fully illustrated, child-tested art activity, featuring painting, drawing, sculpture, photography, architecture, and more.

CHAPTER ELEVEN: SCHEDULES AND RESOURCES FOR CLASSICAL EDUCATION

Henle, Robert J. *Henle Latin.* Chicago: Loyola University Press, 1958.
Originally published in 1945, the Henle Latin series teaches Latin the traditional way. It can be attempted by students with no Latin background as early as seventh grade. Grammar and syntax are collected into a separate Grammar Manual, which is used as a reference for all four years of Henle. The texts contain all of the exercises and readings.

Leithart, Peter J. *Brightest Heaven of Invention: A Christian Guide to Six Shakespeare Plays.* Moscow, ID: Canon Press, 1996.
Shakespeare was a great observer who was able to see deeply into the patterns of human character. Leithart's perceptive walk through six Shakespeare plays is written especially for a high school–level course, but older students will benefit as well.

———. *Heroes of the City of Man.* Moscow, ID: Canon Press, 1999.
Leithart evaluates classic literary works including *The Iliad* and *The Odyssey.* In each, he points out important literary elements, but he also brings out insightful character studies and an examination of the worldviews presented in each work.

Mohs, Karen. *Latin's Not So Tough!* Moline, IL: Greek 'n' Stuff, 1996.
This series lives up to its name. It is a good introduction to Latin that makes foreign language studies as approachable as possible. Available in Levels 1–6.

Trumbull, H. Clay. *Hints on Child Training.* Eugene, OR: Great Expectations Book Co., 1993.
Though not related to language studies specifically, Trumbull gives great ideas on how to talk to children so they can understand an adult's expectations. This book made me a nicer parent and my children able to respond with more maturity to a list of instructions.

Ultimate Spanish: Basic-Intermediate. New York: Living Language, 1998.
  Developed by the experts at Living Language, this deluxe course has everything you need to speak, understand, read, and write Spanish. Ultimate Spanish combines conversation with grammar and culture in an easy-to-follow,
  enjoyable, and effective format. Contains forty lessons; includes eight CDs.

Pogue, David, and Scott Speck. Foreword by Glen Dicterow. *Classical Music for Dummies.* Hoboken, NJ: John Wiley & Sons, 1997.
  This is a down-to-earth guide that will help you get the most out of classical
  music and identify different styles, genres, and modes of classical music. The
  book comes with a CD of classical masterpieces. The book also provides
  links to classical music sites and chat groups on the Internet.

Rhodes, Suzanne. *The Roar on the Other Side: A Guide for Student Poets.* Moscow, ID:
  Canon Press, 2000.
  This book is an invaluable introduction to the habits and skills that make a
  poet, and, to the "vision" that makes a poet worth reading.

Suggested Classic Literature

This list, though certainly not complete, is a great place to start your introduction to
classic literature. You'll see that many of the books listed here are available in Dover
Thrift Editions. Almost any classic that has moved into the public domain is carried by
this publisher. Each book costs only a few dollars and is usually the original version.

Austen, Jane. *Pride and Prejudice.* Mineola, NY: Dover, 1995.
Beowulf. Trans. R. K. Gordon. Mineola, NY: Dover, 1992.
Bunyan, John. *The Pilgrim's Progress.* Mineola, NY: Dover, 2003.
Burnett, Frances Hodgson. *The Secret Garden.* Mineola, NY: Dover, 1994.
Carroll, Lewis. *Alice's Adventures in Wonderland.* Mineola, NY: Dover, 1993.
Colum, Padraic. *The Children's Homer: The Adventures of Odysseus and the Tale of Troy.*
  New York: Simon Pulse, 1982.
Crane, Stephen. *The Red Badge of Courage.* Mineola, NY: Dover, 1990.
Defoe, Daniel. *Robinson Crusoe.* Mineola, NY: Dover, 1998.
Dickens, Charles. *A Christmas Carol.* Mineola, NY: Dover, 1991.
Elliot, Elisabeth. *Through Gates of Splendor.* Carol Stream, IL: Tyndale House, 1981.
Forbes, Esther. *Johnny Tremain.* New York: Yearling, 1987.
Latham, Jean Lee. *Carry On, Mr. Bowditch.* San Anselmo, CA: Sandpiper, 1955.
Lee, Harper. *To Kill a Mockingbird.* New York: Grand Central Publishing, 1988.
London, Jack. *The Call of the Wild.* Mineola, NY: Dover, 1990.
———. *White Fang.* Mineola, NY: Dover, 1991.
Longfellow, Henry Wadsworth. *Favorite Poems.* Mineola, NY: Dover, 1992.
Lowry, Lois. *Number the Stars.* New York: Laurel Leaf, 1998.
Orwell, George. *Animal Farm.* New York: Signet, 2004.

Poe, Edgar Allan. *The Gold-Bug and Other Tales.* Mineola, NY: Dover, 1991.

Rawls, Wilson. *Where the Red Fern Grows.* New York: Laurel Leaf, 1997.

Shakespeare, William. *The Taming of the Shrew.* Mineola, NY: Dover, 1997.

Sir Gawain and the Green Knight. Trans. Bernard O'Donoghue. New York: Penguin, 2007.

Speare, Elizabeth George. *The Bronze Bow.* San Anselmo, CA: Sandpiper, 1997.

———. *The Sign of the Beaver.* New York: Yearling, 1984.

Stevenson, Robert Louis. *Treasure Island.* Mineola, NY: Dover, 1993.

Ten Boom, Corrie. *The Hiding Place.* New York: Bantam Books, 1984.

Tolkien, J. R. R. *The Hobbit.* Boston, MA: Mariner Books, 1999.

Twain, Mark. *The Adventures of Tom Sawyer.* Mineola, NY: Dover, 1998.

Washington, Booker T. *Up from Slavery.* Mineola, NY: Dover, 1995.

Yates, Elizabeth. *Amos Fortune, Free Man.* New York: Puffin, 1989.

INDEX